Pennsylvania Dutch Cook Book

J. GEORGE FREDERICK

DOVER PUBLICATIONS, INC.

NEW YORK

Pennsylvania Dutch Cook Book, first published by Dover Publications, Inc., in 1971, is an unabridged republication of Part II, "Cookery," of *The Pennsylvania Dutch and their Cookery,* as originally published by The Business Bourse in 1935.

International Standard Book Number: 0-486-22676-X
Library of Congress Catalog Card Number: 77-140227

Manufactured in the United States of America
Dover Publications, Inc.
180 Varick Street
New York, N. Y. 10014

Contents

CONVERSION TABLES FOR FOREIGN EQUIVALENTS

DRY INGREDIENTS

Ounces	Grams	Grams	Ounces	Pounds	Kilograms	Kilograms	Pounds
1 =	28.35	1 =	0.035	1 =	0.454	1 =	2.205
2	56.70	2	0.07	2	0.91	2	4.41
3	85.05	3	0.11	3	1.36	3	6.61
4	113.40	4	0.14	4	1.81	4	8.82
5	141.75	5	0.18	5	2.27	5	11.02
6	170.10	6	0.21	6	2.72	6	13.23
7	198.45	7	0.25	7	3.18	7	15.43
8	226.80	8	0.28	8	3.63	8	17.64
9	255.15	9	0.32	9	4.08	9	19.84
10	283.50	10	0.35	10	4.54	10	22.05
11	311.85	11	0.39	11	4.99	11	24.26
12	340.20	12	0.42	12	5.44	12	26.46
13	368.55	13	0.46	13	5.90	13	28.67
14	396.90	14	0.49	14	6.35	14	30.87
15	425.25	15	0.53	15	6.81	15	33.08
16	453.60	16	0.57				

LIQUID INGREDIENTS

Liquid Ounces	Milliliters	Milliliters	Liquid Ounces	Quarts	Liters	Liters	Quarts
1 =	29.573	1 =	0.034	1 =	0.946	1 =	1.057
2	59.15	2	0.07	2	1.89	2	2.11
3	88.72	3	0.10	3	2.84	3	3.17
4	118.30	4	0.14	4	3.79	4	4.23
5	147.87	5	0.17	5	4.73	5	5.28
6	177.44	6	0.20	6	5.68	6	6.34
7	207.02	7	0.24	7	6.62	7	7.40
8	236.59	8	0.27	8	7.57	8	8.45
9	266.16	9	0.30	9	8.52	9	9.51
10	295.73	10	0.33	10	9.47	10	10.57

Gallons (American)	Liters	Liters	Gallons (American)
1 =	3.785	1 =	0.264
2	7.57	2	0.53
3	11.36	3	0.79
4	15.14	4	1.06
5	18.93	5	1.32
6	22.71	6	1.59
7	26.50	7	1.85
8	30.28	8	2.11
9	34.07	9	2.38
10	37.86	10	2.74

1

Regional Cookery
and the Pennsylvania Dutch

IF YOU travel into the South, or into New England, or into Pennsylvania Dutch country, *can you find the cookery of these regions?* The alarming truth is that you *cannot,* unless you are a good hunter, or lucky. Mostly you will get the indifferent, standardized American food, and few indeed are the places where regional cookery pride is maintained. Yet the traditional regional cookery standards of these regions, still known to a limited few, are far above the common food commonly served there now.

The whole United States—speaking in terms of food—is rapidly being rolled over by the broad steam roller of standardization. Rapid transportation, national advertising and the desire of the young to imitate Paris and New York are the causes. The day of regional differences in food is so swiftly passing that the historians of the delectable dishes of various parts of the country are encountering much difficulty. The younger people of the past two generations have not been interested. They want to eat only what everybody else eats. The old people who had the secrets of old cookery have been dying off.

Regional cookery sprang out of regional isolation, and as isolation ends, regional cookery too tends to disappear. This definitely means, in some respects, *deterioration*. It is necessary to work fast if historians are to be able to do anything but pick over the dry bones of inadequate old records and the uncertain memories of octogenarians. The practiced old hands at such cookery are now alarmingly few. It is part of the modern sophistication for young women to go to business rather than to learn what their mothers knew about cookery. From the point of view of regional cookery this is a grave misfortune. This is true even of New England and Southern cookery, which, together with the Pennsylvania Dutch cookery, form the most authentic triumvirate of regional foods in the U. S. There is no disappointment so aggravating as to visit in a land of long-reputed good cookery and be served poor ordinary food.

Pennsylvania Dutch cookery has been the most lamentably neglected of all. There are volumes written about New England and Southern cookery, but except for a few purely local pamphlets and books, Pennsylvania Dutch food is represented in most peoples' minds by only a few superlatively good things—Philadelphia scrapple, Shaker dried corn, Reading pretzels, Philadelphia pepper pot soup, Berks cup cheese, Lebanon sausages, etc. Yet these are only single items in a very considerable repertoire of special cookery, ranging literally from soup to nuts. On the whole the Pennsylvania Dutch is a regional cookery which I think need bow the knee to only one other regional cookery repertoire, namely the Southern. Without disparaging New England cookery, it is true that it has a definitely more narrow range than Southern or Pennsylvania Dutch. The number of dishes peculiar alone to New England is much less than those peculiar alone to the Pennsylvania Dutch cookery. Southern cookery, inclusive of the sub-regional specialties of Maryland, Virginia, South Carolina and Louisiana, is admittedly a very extensive regimen of food and special dishes. Nothing else in all America can compare; on this all authorities agree.

But if one faces the fact that the Pennsylvania Dutch territory comprises only five or six counties of the Keystone state; that it is a mere tiny fraction of land in comparison with Southern territory, or with New England territory, it becomes clear that no other similar small piece of territory in the entire United States ever acquired so notable a reputation in gastronomy. It may be that we must say that New Orleans, as a concentrated spot, holds the greatest laurels, but after New Orleans the Pennsylvania Dutch must surely rate; its five cities (Philadelphia, Reading Lancaster, Allentown, Bethlehem) being the inter-related capitals of Pennsylvania Dutch cookery—although the rest of it is in the country surrounding these cities—each with some individual features, but all united through other features. There is a unity achieved in Pennsylvania Dutch cookery not boasted by any other regional cookery.

It will prove to be a distinct national loss if the careless ways of modern American generations succeed in plowing under all regional cookery, everywhere. The national spirit, the national yardstick of sophistication, the nationizing forces of commerce, education, and transportation, and especially the great addition of foods available out of season and from afar,—all these have made most of our younger generations indifferent, in regions historically notable for cookery.

Fortunately this callow phase is to some extent passing. We are awakening to our local heritages. In the past ten years there has been more attention paid to regional cookery than in fifty years before. Men and women who had considered dull and matter-of-fact the regional foods of their earlier life are now opening their eyes (as they become adult and literate with regard to food, and after traveling abroad, and in the rest of America, or living in large cities). They see that their regional, traditional foods were precious, rich traditions; a pyramid of the skill of countless generations, highly individual and often also highly delectable. The Southern girl who during her school days complained about corn pone, now in sophisticated New York delights to make it for her admiring friends. The New Englander who considered his beans a dull food, may learn (like the late Cyrus Curtis, the famous publisher, born in Maine) to place New England baked beans at the top of all his food preferences. Similarly the Pennsylvania Dutchman who perhaps scowled as a youth when his mother too often served him scrapple, now (like the famous writer Joseph Hergesheimer, a Dutchman himself) smacks his lips over it, boasts of it, and sniffs indignantly when *Vogue* mistakenly calls scrapple "hash."

It is all somewhat like the habit of upstanding American men to leave their homes early, to be impatient, scornful, and eager to go to far places—only to return a little later in life, enraptured with a new appreciation of the old homestead—like Owen D. Young, famous industrialist, who has gone back to Hornellsville, N. Y.; or like Henry Ford, who is spending millions to re-create the scenes of his early boyhood. So it is with regional cookery which has basic merit. Those who were reared in the regions of America where a real cookery tradition prevailed may leave the board of their mothers, but they suffer often a gastronomic disillusionment elsewhere, for their palates never lose the thrill of those original delights, which seemed in restless childhood to be uninteresting. Even if they fall victim of the Parisian siren, and worship at the feet of Brillat-Savarin and Escoffier—famous masters of the French cuisine, now supreme around the world—still, they almost surely come some day to the point when their palates turn homeward bound again.

If they acquire real food discrimination they do not over-value any cuisine—including their own regional one. They acquire a real individual approach to food; one suited to themselves; one capable of sifting all cuisines to eliminate the over-elaborate or unsuitable, and yet one capable of appreciating at least a portion of the regional dishes of America.

Lucky indeed they are if they have New England, Southern or Pennsylvania Dutch regional food memories of feasts of many kinds, and for this reason have acquired, almost unconsciously, a higher standard of taste. I have a theory that those people who were not born and fed in regions which had special culinary prides and repertoires, *virtually never acquire any real food discrimination.* They will placidly eat "railroad station pie" or drink "coffee shop slop" all their lives without rebellion; scarcely knowing that they are entitled to something better. Their palates have been ruined during the impressionable period of youth, and food never matters much to them thereafter, except as necessary nourishment.

Not so the regional person who was cooked for by someone inheriting regional cookery pride and skill. Something is swallowed with such food which conditions a person for a life-time, even though there may be interim periods of indifference. A standard has been set; a memory etched; a yardstick of food delight notched accurately, by which all other food ever taken will be measured infallibly. Possibly this explains why the two foremost newspaper food editors in New York—Edith Barber of the *Sun,* and Esther E. Kimmel, head of the *Herald-Tribune* Home Institute, are Pennsylvania Dutch.

Pennsylvania Dutch cookery stems of course from the German, for "Pennsylvania Dutch" is a colloquialism for Pennsylvania German. As Prof. Cornelius Weygandt says, however "it is pedantry and worse than pedantry to insist on 'Pennsylvania German'." There is every sound basis for preferring the colloquial terms; indeed there was some Holland Dutch in the early emigration. The Pennsylvania Dutch, coming from the storied Rhine Valley, the Palatinate, and even from German Switzerland, brought with them the very best and most individual German cookery. And, as Henry T. Finck, America's greatest gourmet, was wont to say, Parisian cookery has been a little over-advertised as the world's greatest cuisine; the German cuisine ranking very close, indeed.

Thus the Dutch of Pennsylvania, arriving even before 1700, have had centuries in which to adapt German culinary skill to the American situation; and since the French nowhere except in New Orleans set up their high standards in early America, these

Pennsylvania Dutch standards quite logically rank with those of the French colony in America. The locale determined the fundamental differences. In New Orleans seafood was superabundant, and thus we have New Orleans cookery almost concentrated upon it. It was a hot country, too, and therefore, as in all hot countries, high spicing was the rule. Moreover, New Orleans was *a city.*

In the Pennsylvania Dutch country a quite different situation prevailed, even though Delaware shad and oysters were fairly plentiful at the lower edge of the territory. The prevailing mode of life was *rural,* and fairly sparsely settled, too. The Dutch farm was more or less isolated, and from a food point of view had to be self-sustaining. The Dutch cuisine, therefore, based itself upon a farm technique; which for winter foods had to depend upon preserves, dried and smoked foods and those provisions which could be stored for many months. (Some people think the dried apple which the early Dutch used extensively, was disdained elsewhere. In Mac Master's *History of the People of the U.S.* he tells how beef, pork, salt fish and dried apples "were the daily fare in Boston about 1800 from one year's end to another.")

This was a superb culinary challenge. The palate's long winter tedium could only be relieved, first by great agility in gathering, preserving and storing foods for the winter, and second by exceptional skill in cooking those foods and developing variety by combination. For this reason the Pensylvania Dutch farm from 1700 to 1900—two full centuries—and on a number of farms even today—was made into a food factory of amazing scope and range. I have attempted in a later chapter to describe this graphically by depicting a full season, from May to December, on the farm of my grandparents, whom during the late eighties I visited frequently as a small boy.

The Pennsylvania Dutch have never been accused of being undernourished or badly fed. Their diet was, from our modern sedentary point of view, perhaps rather too lusty and hospitable in earlier days, and from the point of view of modern out-of-season food facilities too limited during winter days—but this was no fault of the Dutch. Florida lettuce, Texas broccoli and California oranges were not delivered to a 1735 farm door in February, as in 1935! We are a very spoiled people today in regard to food, and inclined to discount clever cookery in favor of sheer variety.

Furthermore, it is true, as in the South and in New England, that very few individuals were ever master of the whole range of Dutch cookery. Each one of the Pennsylvania counties (and even parts of counties) had specialties of their own; and indeed preferences, dislikes, habits and disadvantages of their own. For these reasons the very best of Dutch cooks have usually been limited in their repertoire. This book represents *the very first time in two and one half centuries of Dutch history* when practically the entire repertoire of Dutch cookery was brought together. Even so, I have omitted a number of recipes which have been current somewhere in Dutch-land at one time or another—largely because they are of no particular modern interest.

To an increasing degree Pennsylvania Dutch cookery (as in the case of Dutch furniture and pottery, etc.) is being accorded recognition, and I predict a still greater degree of interest. The liking for Scrapple, Philadelphia Pepperpot Soup, Reading pretzels, etc. is now more or less national, and still other items may become equally so. In her Fifth Avenue, New York restaurant and shop Mary Elizabeth recently made a window display of her old Pennsylvania Dutch family recipes and proudly boasted that some of her specialties were made from them.

In the Dutch country itself there is arising an insistence that there be available country and wayside inns and restaurants where the old Dutch cookery might be found.

Until several decades ago there were several famous Dutch gourmet paradises, especially near Reading. Operating for years in a secluded nook on Mt. Penn, close by Reading, "Kuechler's Roost" acquired fame in half a dozen states. To this restaurant came famous people from all over Pennsylvania and elsewhere.

Old Kuechler was given high praise for his Dutch dishes by men who had dined at the best places of the world. Unfortunately Kuechler's death and the depression ended this famous gourmet's retreat. The same fate overtook Carl Schaich's and Frank Lauer's places near Reading, also Steigerwald's and Spuhler's. In Philadelphia, Lancaster and Allentown similar misfortunes overtook old gourmet retreats; but as even famous old restaurants in Paris are meeting the same fate (as for example Voisin's and Montagne's and Ciro's), it is not to be wondered at.

The old inns in Dutch-land also dropped Dutch cookery about a dozen years ago, stupidly believing that the American cookery level of the wayside stand was all that was wanted. But there is developing a new food consciousness demanding some of the unsurpassed cookery of old Dutch days. Some intelligent hotels and restaurants are seeing their new opportunity.

While Dutch regional cookery is not, in my opinion, without some faults and limitations, this is true of any other regional cookery, even the southern; but the recipes in this book should make clear why Dutch cookery in my humble opinion, has points of superiority to *any* regional cookery in America.

2

Pennsylvania Dutch Soups

L IKE OTHER European peoples, except the French and English the Dutch often relied upon a good soup to make the main dish of the meal.

A really quite astounding variety of unique soups is presented here. Some of these soups are very rich, but others could well be called— (indeed have been called) —*poverty soups.*

In those long pioneer years from 1700 onward, when the Dutch homesteads had to be operated with iron economy, the ingenuity of the Dutch *hausfrau* came to the fore to produce some singularly cheap and yet singularly flavorful soups.

The Brown Flour Soup (*Braune Mehlsuppe*) is distinctive of these, and I well remember that during the 1893 panic when my parents had to feed six children on very little income indeed, I was very frequently fed this soup; also the Dutch Potato Soup; also the Brown Potato Chowder; a kind of combination of both. All good cooks will agree that flour carefully browned develops a very appetizing flavor; it is the very source of the appetizing appeal of bread or pie crust, so why shouldn't it be good? I can relish it today. The Potato Soup, Brown Chowder, and the Pretzel Soup days in my home were always good days for me!

The Dutch masterpiece, Philadelphia Pepperpot Soup, was already on its way to being nationalized before the Campbell's Soup concern (with its great factories right in the Dutch territory) made it international by canning it. It is made with some local variations, but it is a man's soup in superlative degree. The ladies sometimes complain that it is too "hot," but men would not do away with the cayenne in it. I provide two recipes from different counties.

The Dutch make, of course, such standard things as vegetable, bean and noodle soup, but their noodles when home-made are not the fine-cut Hungarian type; they are broader and thicker. They also use soup balls and egg drops in soup broth.

Clam soup was not a frequent treat for the Dutch, but it was liked.

1
Philadelphia Snapper Soup

1 snapper turtle	3 stalks celery
1 gallon beef or chicken broth	6 tomatoes
½ lb. chicken fat or lard	1 hard boiled egg
4 lbs. veal knuckle	2 cups sherry
1 carrot	3 slices lemon
3 onions	1 cup flour
½ teaspoon marjoram	3 cloves
2 bay leaves	salt and pepper

When buying the veal have it broken into two-inch pieces. Place in bake pan, together with carrot, onions, celery, diced, and the fat. Add all the spices and cook in hot oven. When brown, sprinkle over it the flour and put back to brown again. Then transfer to a soup pot, add the broth, chop the tomatoes, and add cover and boil for 3½ to 4 hours. Then dice the turtle meat, place in pan to simmer for 5 minutes with one half of the sherry, lemon slices, salt and tabasco. Then remove the lemon and mix the turtle with the soup after straining. Then chop the boiled egg and add, together with the other half of the sherry.

2
Philadelphia Pepper Pot Soup

1 veal joint	½ lb. beef suet
4 pounds tripe	2 bay leaves
2 onions	2 teaspoons salt
1 bunch herbs	1 teaspoon black pepper
4 potatoes	½ teaspoon cayenne pepper
2 teaspoons of minced parsley	1 red pepper
1 cup beef suet	2 cups flour

This is a two-day job of cookery.

Scrape tripe, wash in three waters (cold). Put in cold water to boil for 7 or 8 hours, then after tripe is cool cut into ½ inch squares. The next day simmer for 3 hours the veal with bones in 3 quarts of cold water; and skim off the scum. Separate meat from bones and dice. Strain the broth, add bay leaves, chopped onions, and simmer for another hour. Add then the potatoes, diced, the herbs, parsley and red pepper, cut. Add the meat, salt, cayenne, add also dumplings made of the beef suet flour and salt, mixed, and made to a paste consistency with cold water. Roll in flour the dumplings, only ½ inch in diameter. Drop into soup and simmer five minutes more.

3
Dutch Eel Soup

3 eels	1 small bunch parsley roots
4 tablespoons butter	8 egg yolks
½ cup sherry	1 teaspoon minced parsley
6 dozen small shrimp (or tails of larger shrimp)	1 teaspoon lemon juice
3 pints blond of veal	Cayenne pepper (or paprika) ;
1 tablespoon minced blanched parsley	salt, thyme, bay leaf, sweet basil, several pepper corns, blade of mace
1 stalk celery	3 carrots
1 shallot	1 cup mushrooms (canned)

After filleting the eel, cut into small scallops. Arrange these scallops in circles in large fry-pan in which the butter has been melted and sprinkled over with the cayenne pepper (or paprika), the lemon juice, parsley and salt added. Simmer for 20 minutes, then add sherry, after which bring to boil for two minutes. Put the eel scallops into a soup tureen, together with 3 dozen of the shrimp, and pour over it immediately a soup sauce prepared as follows: dice carrots, celery, shallot, mushrooms, parsley roots. Fry until brown the thyme, bay leaf, sweet basil, pepper corns, mace, using two tablespoons of butter; then put in the eel-bones and eel trimmings also the other 3 dozen shrimp. Boil for five minutes, add the veal. Then let boil gently for 45 minutes, strain vigorously through cheese cloth. Pour this broth into a stew pan, thicken with white flour to consistency of a quite thin sauce. Add the eight egg yolks, and the blanched parsley. It is then ready to pour into the soup tureen.

4
Dutch Wine Soup

¾ cup rice	2 qts. water
2 lbs. sweet-sour apples	½ lemon
¼ teaspoon salt	1 cup sugar
½ pt. white wine	

Wash and boil the rice in 2 cups of water for 5 minutes. Pour off the water and add 2 qts. Boil one hour. Peel and core the apples, cut them up in eighths, and put into rice. Also cut up the lemon in slices and add to the soup. Boil all this 20 minutes after adding salt and sugar.

If the soup is too thick, add some more water. Serve hot or cold.

5
Dutch Raspberry Sago Soup

3 cups water	¼ cup sago
2 slices lemon	½ cup sugar
1½ cups raspberry juice	

Soak the sago in cold water for an hour; then pour off the water and add 3 cups of fresh water. Boil until soft and transparent. Add the raspberry juice, sugar and lemon and let boil 5 minutes longer. Remove the lemon slices. Serve this soup with Dutch Butter Pretzels.

(Jenny Lind, famous singer, was exceedingly fond of sago soup and attributed her good health to it.)

6
Dutch Green Corn Soup

1½ cups green corn	1 tablespoon butter
3 qts. bouillon	1 or 2 yolks of eggs
¼ lb. Dutch Butter Pretzels	

Steep the green corn in the butter, then add the bouillon; boil slowly for 2 hours. Strain through a fine sieve, and stir in the yolk of one egg.

Serve with Dutch Butter Pretzels (which can be broken into small pieces into the soup before serving, or served one pretzel to each plate).

7
Dutch Apple Soup

2 lbs. apples	2 qts. water
¼ lb. sugar	1 stick of cinnamon
2 tablespoons cornstarch	1/8 lb. currants
Juice of ½ lemon and a small piece of rind	

Do not pare the apples; core and cut into pieces, then boil in water with the spices until soft. Mix the flour with a little water and add while boiling. Strain through a sieve, add the washed currants, and a cup of red wine or white wine, and cook again. Serve hot or cold. Other fruit soups may be made, with strawberries, raspberries, currants, grapes, gooseberries, rhubarb, plum or cherry. The Dutch even use dried apples or other dried fruits sometimes.

8
Rye Bread Soup

2 lbs. rye bread	2 qts. water
Salt	1 tumbler full of white wine
Sugar	1 tablespoon fresh butter

½ cup currants

Use stale rye bread, with 2 qts. of cold water. Boil a little, then press through a fine sieve.

If it should be too thick, leave out some bread. Boil with the salt, sugar, currants, and butter for a little while. Pour the white wine into the soup dish, and then pour in the soup, boiling hot, on top of it.

9
Fish Soup With Fish Dumplings

2½ lbs. pickerel or other fish	1½ qts. water
½ onion	Salt
1/8 lb. flour	1/8 lb. butter
1 qt. bouillon	8 oysters
15 shrimps or crab meat	1/8 qt. white wine
2 tablespoons butter	2 yolks of eggs

12 small fish dumplings

Clean the fish, cut meat from the bones, remove the liver and gall. Chop up the bones and put in the water, with onions salt and spices. Slowly stew to make fish bouillon.

Melt the quarter pound of butter, stir in the flour, simmer to a light yellow, pour the fish bouillon in, let it simmer slowly for 45 minutes. Boil the crabs or crawfish in the meantime, take the meat out of the shells. Heat in the white wine (but do not boil), the oysters and the fish liver, cut into pieces. Cut the meat of the pickerel into small pieces and stew in 2 tablespoonfuls of butter until tender.

Make the dumplings of fish, using 1 cup fish, 1 egg, ½ cup crust crumbs, 1 teaspoon butter, ½ teaspoon minced parsley, one teaspoon salt. Beat the egg whites. Cook the fish dumplings also 10 minutes in the white wine, then put them into the soup tureen; also all the meat, liver, crabs and oysters. Strain the gravy, stir in the yolks of 2 eggs, and then pour into the tureen. Salt to taste.

10
Oysterplant Soup

2 bundles oysterplants   2½ tablespoons butter
2 tablespoons flour   2 yolks of eggs
                1½ qts. milk

Clean and scrape the oysterplants, and dice into inch pieces— after which at once put them into water mixed with vinegar and flour so that they will not darken.

Stew them with the butter and a little water until tender; then stir in the flour and cook a few minutes. Then add the milk gradually stirring constantly. Let cook a little, stirring occasionally, and then add salt and pepper, and finally stir in the yolks of 2 eggs.

11
Dutch Black Soup (Schwarz Sauer)

Giblets of 1 goose or duck   ¼ lb. prunes
¼ cup of sugar   1 small stick of cinnamon
½ lb. of peeled apples or pears 2 cloves
4 pepper-corns   Scant 1 pt. of goose or duck
1½ tablespoons vinegar   blood
2 tablespoons flour   1½ qts. water

Use neck, head, feet, wings, heart, gizzard of goose or duck, well cleaned. Cook until tender in 1 qt. of water with salt, pepper and 2 cloves. Cook the prunes and apples or pears (quartered) in a pint of water. Stir the blood with the flour into one-half of the broth from the giblets, and pour back on again. Add the chopped fruit, then season with vinegar and sugar and bring to boil, stirring constantly to prevent coagulation.

12
Dutch Potato Soup

Pare and dice four large potatoes, boil in 1 quart of water until soft. Take ½ lb. of fat meat, cut into tiny pieces and fry. (If meat is very fat, pour off part of the drippings.) Take 2 medium sized onions, slice, and fry with the meat until soft and brown, and pour into the potatoes.

Take cup sour cream mixed with one well beaten egg. Pour this mixture into the potatoes, meat and onions. Stir well, add enough vinegar to give sour taste, add more salt if necessary, let all come to a good boil. Serve hot immediately after the soup is made.

13
Dutch Chicken Corn Soup

Boil chicken until tender, remove bones and shred meat; make a smooth dough of one egg and one and one-half cups of flour; roll out and cut into dice; score and cut off the corn from six ears; put all into the chicken broth and boil together till corn is soft. Serve with popcorn floating on the soup.

14
Cider Soup

Boil there pints of cider, skim, put one-half cup sugar in cider, take two cups of bread cut in dice, brown in butter, take two eggs, beat well, add two tablespoonfuls of sugar, two tablespoonfuls of flour, one and one-half cups of milk, few whole allspice, add to boiling cider. Stir browned bread in mixture last.

15
Egg Soup

Crumb stale bread until you have as much as is desired and brown in plenty of butter. Do not have the bread too fine and stir it continually while browning. Then bake one egg over browned bread and stir a short time longer. Remove into tureen and pour water into pan, salting well, and when it boils pour over bread. Have enough to cover and eat at once.

16
Calf's Head Soup

1 calf's head	½ teaspoon cloves
1 lb. chopped veal	2 large tablespoons browned
5 eggs	flour
1 teaspoon sweet marjoram	

Wash head, remove brains and let stand in salt water a half hour. Boil for 10 or 12 minutes, until meat is tender. Then strain; cut meat fine, and add browned flour, the eggs (hard-boiled and chopped fine), butter balls. Also balls made of force-meat, using 1 lb. chopped veal, 1 raw egg, little melted butter, seasoning. Mold into balls and fry in butter. Butter balls are made by mixing 1 cup flour with 1/2 cup butter and 1/2 teaspoon salt, and moistening with ice water, shape into balls, and boil ten minutes.

17
Brown Potato Soup

1 quart milk, 4 medium sized potatoes, 2 tablespoons flour, 1 tablespoon butter, 1 hard boiled egg. Dice potatoes and boil in water until tender, add milk. Brown flour in butter, add to the hot mixture, and boil a few minutes until it thickens. Season for taste.

18
Rivel Soup

1 quart milk, 1 egg, 1 cup flour; mix egg and flour, and rub thru hands in small lumps, and let shreds drop into boiling milk. Cook about five minutes.

19
Milk Corn Soup

Peel and shred a quarter of a cabbage, and add 2 tomatoes. Cover with water and cook until tender. Take six ears of corn, slit the kernels and scrape (whole grains are not desirable and grated is too fine.) In another vessel heat 1 quart of milk, 1/4 pound of butter, 1/4 teaspoon baking soda, salt. When hot, add to the other mixture. Cook up slowly, (it burns easily). Then add butter balls made with ¾ cup of flour, 1 teaspoon butter—water to soften, ½ teaspoon baking powder, and a bit of salt. Toss bits of dough into flour, drop into hot soup for ten minutes, slowly cooking. Add 2 hard boiled eggs, parsley and serve with popcorn floating on it.

20
Dutch Pretzel Soup

2 lbs. Reading butter pretzels (on sale throughout the East)	2 cups water
	3 tablespoons butter
4 cups rich milk	2 tablespoons flour

Salt, pepper, juice of parsley

Blend butter and flour. Combine milk and water and heat. Stir blended butter with milk until creamy and smooth. Season. Pour into serving dish. Break pretzels into small pieces and add just before serving. Combine with juice of parsley. Serves 6.

21
Dutch Navy Bean Soup

2 lbs. navy beans	2 tablespoons flour
1 pork shank or bacon end	2 tablespoons butter
Leeks,	3 potatoes

Cloves, salt, pepper.

Put the navy beans in lukewarm water for 12 hours. Place the pork or bacon in the bottom of pot and put in beans, leeks, five cloves, salt, pepper. Then scorch the flour with the butter in hot pan, add some of the bean stock and put in the pot and boil until beans are tender. Boil the potatoes separately, dice, and add just before serving hot.

22
Dutch Lettuce Soup

3 heads iceberg lettuce	Beef broth
2 tablespoons butter, or chicken fat	2 tablespoons rice
	1 teaspoon sugar
1 tablespoon flour	1 cup light cream

Salt, Pepper.

Wash the lettuce thoroughly, dry them with a clean towel or napkin. Chop moderately fine, and then stew for 5 minutes, together with the fat mixed previously with the flour. Then add the rice, salt and beef broth sufficient for sewing. Cook for 60 minutes. Strain, blend with the cream, and serve with croutons, small pieces of Dutch pretzels, or popcorn, or with some of the soup dumplings described elsewhere.

23
Dutch Calf's Liver Soup

$\frac{1}{2}$ lb. calf's liver	1 teaspoon minced parsley
3 eggs	$\frac{1}{2}$ teaspoon sugar
3 tablespoons bread crumbs, soup stock	3 tablespoons peas or asparagus tips
1 onion	

Mince finely the calf's liver, mashing it through fine colander. Add the onion minced browned in butter, with a little salt and pepper and parsley. Gradually stir in the yolks and the egg-whites, beaten. Pour into buttered tin and bake golden in medium oven. Let cool and cut into small rings and diamond shapes. Serve with hot clear soup, into which peas or asparagus tips are added.

24

Dutch Corn Chowder

¼ lb. salt pork	2 tablespoons flour
1 onion	1 teaspoon celery salt
¼ lb. Shaker dried corn (or canned or fresh corn)	½ teaspoon paprika
4 potatoes	½ teaspoon pepper, salt to taste
	1 quart milk

Soak the shaker corn for 18 to 24 hours in lukewarm water.

Cut pork into little cubes and fry golden brown. Mince the onion and fry until brown. Pare and dice the potatoes and cook with the pork and bacon in water to cover, pulp the corn, mix with the spices and the milk, and add 6 to 7 soda crackers which have been soaked in milk.

25

Dutch Chicken Chowder

Remains of chicken	2 tablespoons flour
1 quart milk	1 small onion
3 potatoes	1 tablespoon salt pork or bacon
2 tablespoons butter	

Use the remains of a chicken meal, separate from bones and dice. Place bones in cold water together with left-over gravy and simmer for 30 minutes. Strain, add the milk (a quart for each quart of broth).

Mince the onion and brown with the salt pork or bacon, diced, add the potatoes, parboiled and diced, the butter and flour, and simmer further. Season to taste, serve hot, with water crackers or Dutch butter pretzels.

26
Dutch Chestnut Soup

1 cup mashed chestnuts	1 tablespoon flour
1 cup mashed lentils	1½ teaspoons onion juice
1 cup cream	½ tablespoon minced parsley
5 cups soup stock	½ cup minced celery
1 cup diced sausage	2 tablespoons butter
(Lebanon bologna, smoked	1 teaspoon salt
beef or frankfurter)	

After melting the butter in a cooking pot, put in the celery and let cook for ten minutes, frequently stirring. After having cooked and mashed the chestnuts, add this and the cooked and mashed lentils, onion juice, parsley, sausages and soup stock. Let simmer for 20 minutes. Dissolve the flour in a little cold milk, add and then bring to a boil. Add the salt. Serve hot with Dutch butter pretzels.

27
Pod Pea Soup, Mennonite

2 quarts green English peas	3 tablespoons butter
(pods only)	1 teaspoon salt
1 onion	1 teaspoon pepper
2 cups milk	3 tablespoons flour
1 teaspoon sugar	a little nutmeg

Wash the pea pods, cut into inch-long pieces, boil in water with onion for 1½ hours. Strain through colander, add pepper, salt, sugar, nutmeg and milk (which has been scalded). Bring to a boil and thicken with butter and flour mixture.

28
Dutch Rice Onion Soup

1 onion	2 eggs
½ cup rice	1½ teaspoons salt
½ cup cream	½ teaspoon pepper
2 tablespoons minced parsley	1 tablespoon flour
½ cup grated Swiss cheese	several grains mace

In 2 quarts of boiling water put the salt and the rice and the onion, minced. Cook rice until soft, add the mace and pepper. Put in the flour mixed in a bit of milk. Beat the eggs and stir in slowly. Whip the cream and add. Serve sprinkled with cheese and parsley.

29

Pepper Pot Soup, Northumberland

1 soup bone	1 teaspoon minced parsley
1 cup flour	celery tops, etc.
1 small red pepper	

Cook the soup bone until tender and rich in broth. Remove the meat and dice it moderately fine. Meantime have ready a paste made of the flour mixed with some water, rolled out thin and dried a little. Cut this into small squares, which put into the broth and cook, together with a small hot red pepper, the parsley, celery tops, or other summer savory. Serve hot.

30

Dutch Vegetable Soup

With Butter Balls

½ head cabbage	1 cup beans
1 soup bone	2 carrots
1 cup tomatoes	½ cup rice
1 can corn	Pepper, salt
½ cup turnips, diced	Butter-balls
	4 potatoes, diced

These are cooked in the broth of the soup above. The butter-balls are merely small dumplings, made as follows: Mix 1 teaspoon of butter with 3 tablespoons of flour, ½ teaspoon of salt, and water, to make a stiff paste. Roll into small balls and boil in the soup for a short time. (These butter balls are good also in calf's-head or other soups.)

31
Spring Vegetable Soup, Mt. Joy

2 small heads lettuce
2 cups green peas
1 onion (minced)
2 teaspoons minced parsley
3 eggs (yolks only)

3 pinks soup stock
2 teaspoons salt
1 teaspoon pepper
2 oz. butter

In a pint of water in a stewpan put the onion, lettuce, parsley and butter and simmer until tender; then add salt and pepper. Strain, and put two-thirds of the liquor into the soup stock. Beat the egg-yolks, toss over hot fire, and when broth is ready to serve, put in the cooked corn and the egg.

32
Dutch Yellow Tomato Soup

1 pint yellow tomatoes
1 pint milk
½ teaspoon baking soda
¼ teaspoon pepper

½ teaspoon paprika
1 tablespoon butter
1 teaspoon salt

Cook the tomatoes, quartered, in a quart of water until soft, then add the milk, salt, pepper and butter. Let come to a boil, then add the baking soda. Pour this over scalded crackers in soup plates and serve hot, with paprika sprinkled over it.

Note: The yellow tomato, as the famous epicure Henry T. Finck asserts in his book *Food and Flavor,* is too much neglected today, yet has a very fine flavor of its own. The Dutch realize this.

33
Dutch Cream Corn Soup

1 quart green corn from cob (or 1 cup Shaker dried corn)
2 stalks celery, diced
1 pint milk
2 teaspoons salt

1 teaspoon pepper
2 tablespoons butter
1 tablespoon cornstarch
3 hard boiled eggs
1 teaspoon minced parsley

If using Shaker corn soak in lukewarm water for about 12 hours. Boil the corn and celery for 20 minutes, then add salt and pepper and the butter, also the cornstarch (dissolved in a little cold water). Boil a little longer and then add the milk, parsley and eggs, cut fine and serve hot.

34

Clam Soup, Chester

25 clams	2 teaspoons salt
3 potatoes	1 teaspoon pepper
1 tablespoon butter	1 teaspoon minced parsley
3 hard-boiled eggs	2 tablespoons flour

Boil the potatoes (diced) in one quart of water for 15 minutes; don't let stick. Add the salt, pepper and parsley, flour and butter and milk. Boil 8 minutes more, then add the clams, chopped, also the eggs, cut fine. Boil another minute. Have ready the strained liquor of the clams, hot, and pour into the soup just before serving. Serve with Dutch butter pretzels.

35

Liver Noodles (Leberknoedel)

(For use with soups)

1 calf's liver	2 eggs
1 onion	$\frac{1}{2}$ cup breadcrumbs
1 tablespoon butter	$\frac{1}{4}$ teaspoon cloves
salt and pepper	$\frac{1}{4}$ teaspoon marjoram

Simmer the liver in boiling water for 30 minutes. Then take from the liver any skin or ligaments, and grind the liver fine. Spice it with the condiments. Mince the onion, add and mix the butter into the paste; also beat the eggs and add them. Work into the paste the bread crumbs, using enough to make the paste stiff. Poach these balls for 15 minutes in whatever soup you are going to serve them, and then serve them, swimming in the soup.

36
Dutch Potato Chowder

5 potatoes
2 tablespoons butter
5 tablespoons flour
½ teaspoon salt

Dash of pepper
¼ teaspoon minced parsley
1 teaspoon butter or lard

Dice the potatoes, stew in a quart of salted water until tender; replenish water to a quart. In a frying pan melt butter, add the flour, stir carefully to avoid scorching until flour is golden brown. Then add the potatoes and the water. Stir until it is of creamy consistency, but do not smash all flour lumps. Do not make it into thin soup consistency; this is a chowder. Add a little minced parsley, a little salt, and pepper and butter.

37
Dutch Bean Chowder

1 lb. cooked or canned beans
2 tablespoons butter
5 tablespoons flour

1 teaspoon salt
½ teaspoon pepper
¼ teaspoon minced parsley

Use beans and the water in which they were cooked, or if canned beans add water and heat. Brown the flour in pan with butter or lard, add the beans and water, keeping to thick consistency, and adding salt, pepper and parsley.

3

Various Dutch Oddities

There are a great many oddities in the Dutch cuisine. The clever Dutch *Hausfrau* made use of many things not ordinarily available, and rang the changes on many familiar foods.

They were particularly intelligent, for instance, about *meat* jellies—aspics as they are often called today. These are not only highly nutritious, but most delectable. In summer time I regard them as being much superior to hot meats. Others of these are described in the meat, fish chapters.

The Pig's Foot Jelly is one of the Dutch masterpieces. It is encountered elsewhere, it is true, but never as in Dutch-land, made by Dutch housewives. It is better seasoned, purer and more carefully selected.

Old-time oddities like Boova Shenkel and Schnecken are too much neglected today. Then the Rabbit Cake (hardly a good description, for it isn't a cake) ; Oyster Croquettes, Stuffed Beef Heart, *Duck Un Kraut.* Stuffed Liver, etc., are all unique and delicious.

38
Boova Shenkel (Dutch Meat Rolls)

2½ lbs. beef
10 or 12 potatoes
2 tablespoons butter
2 tablespoons minced parsley
1 chopped onion
½ cup milk

3 eggs
2½ cups flour
2 teaspoons baking powder
1 tablespoon lard
1 tablespoon butter
½ teaspoon salt

After seasoning the beef with salt and pepper, stew the meat for 2 or 3 hours until thoroughly tender. Then make dough, sifting flour, adding baking powder, salt, lard and butter. Mix into a pie crust dough, roll into a dozen circles of 8 to 10 inches diameter. Steam the potatoes, pared and sliced thin, add salt and pepper, 2 tablespoons butter, the parsley and onion, and then beat lightly the 3 eggs into the mixture. Put this mixture on the circles of dough, after it has stood a little while, roll over and press the pastry edges together tightly along the edge. Drop these into the stew pot with the meat and its stew water. Cover the pot tightly and cook for 30 minutes slowly.

To make a sauce for this, the fat should have been skimmed from the stew-pot before putting in the dough rolls, and this used in a frying pan with a tablespoon of butter to brown diced stale bread croutons, adding half a cup of milk.

39
Schnecken

1 cup milk
1 yeast cake
3 cups flour
¼ cup sugar
¼ cup seeded raisins

1 teaspoon salt
1 egg
1 egg yolk
¼ cup melted butter
½ cup almonds, shredded

First, scald the milk; let stand until luke warm, then add sugar, salt and yeast cake. Let stand 5 minutes and add 1½ cups flour, beat well, cover and let rise until light, add eggs, butter, and only enough flour to knead, and let rise again. Roll dough

½ inch thick, brush with melted butter, sprinkle with sugar and cinnamon mixed, raisins, and almonds. Roll up like jelly roll and cut in 1 inch pieces. Place pieces in pan close together, flat side down. Brush tops with butter, sprinkle with sugar and cinnamon. To give the Schnecken a bun-like stickiness put brown sugar and butter on bottom of pan before putting Schnecken in.

40

Dutch Festival Doughnuts

(Fastnachts)

NOTE: Fastnacht Day, Shrove Tuesday (the last day before Lent begins) has always meant, in Dutch country, the baking of "Fastnachts," a kind of doughnut. It once included a fasting period at some obscure ancient time, but the Dutch never fast! The last Fastnacht Day, March 5, 1935, saw 360,000 Fastnachts made in Lancaster alone.

Boil 3 potatoes in enough water to cover. With the potato water scald 1 pint of flour and add the potato mashed. When cool add 1 Fleischman yeast cake, dissolved in a little luke warm water. Start this about 5 P.M. At bedtime mix a pint of flour with one pint of lukewarm milk. Stir enough flour into milk to make a batter that will drop readily from the spoon. To this batter add the first mixture and let rise over night. In the morning add 4 beaten eggs, ½ cup of melted butter, or butter and lard mixed, and 1 cup of sugar.

Knead stiff enough to roll; let rise till the dough doubles its size. Now roll and cut out the dough and let rise again. When light, swim in hot fat. The Fastnacht makes extra good "dunking" in coffee or molasses, sometimes both!

41

Dutch Stuffed Tripe

½ lb. spare ribs   4 diced potatoes
½ lb. sausage   1 onion

Fill the big stomach (tripe) with the above ingredients and sew up. Boil about 2 hours; then brown in pan with butter.

42

Dutch Ham and Lima Beans

Secure 2 lb. butt of ham (be sure that it is not salty). Cover with water and add 1 lb. of dried lima beans. Cook very slowly three or four hours. Add water if necessary—do not let go dry. When ready to serve there should be a nice heavy liquid. Add 1 ounce of butter and if necessary, ½ teaspoon of cornstarch, so that the gravy with the beans will not be too thin.

43

Dutch Sauerkraut Dumplings

1 egg beaten, ⅛ teaspoon salt, 1 tablespoon milk, ½ cup of flour, ½ teaspoon baking powder. Make into a paste. Drop into boiling kraut.

44

Dutch Filled Noodles

1 lb. sausage (out of the casing), 1 egg, 1 onion, parsley. Mix thoroughly and spread on a 12 inch round of noodle dough rolled very thin. Roll up like jelly roll, cut into three inch pieces, and boil in hot water or meat broth about one half hour.

45

Buttered Noodles

(*Schmeltzde Nudelen*)

Put as many noodles as you want into a kettle of boiling salt water and boil 20 minutes. Drain. Put into your serving dish and pour brown butter over them and scatter croutons over the top. Cut the bread smaller than you would to make croutons for soup.

46

Dutch Stuffing (*Filsel*)

10 large potatoes	1 teaspoon salt
5 slices bread	½ teaspoon pepper
2 cups chopped celery	½ lb. butter
3 medium onions	3 eggs
½ pint milk	

Boil potatoes in the skins; peel and mash with ¼ lb. butter, and add ½ cup milk. Spread the bread with butter, cut in half inch pieces, and brown in the oven on a tray, stirring them several times to brown on all sides. Fry onions and celery in butter. Beat the eggs, and add the whole mixture, stirring and blending it thoroughly. Last of all heat remaining butter and milk, and pour over mixture stirring it well, then put in a buttered glass pie dish, and bake 45 minutes.

47

Grumbera (*Potato*) Dumplings

Grate four raw, cold potatoes; dip 8 slices of bread in water and squeeze. Put bread in stew pan with 1 small grated onion, a little parsley, salt and pepper to taste. Add potatoes and 2 well beaten eggs. Form into balls and roll in flour delicately. Drop in salted boiling water and cook, well covered, for fifteen minutes.

These are excellent to accompany sauerkraut, meat or stewed or fricaseed chicken, or pot roast.

48
Pickled Pig's Feet (Stiderly)

2 pigs feet
1 teaspoon gelatine
½ teaspoon pepper

1 lb. lean pork
1 cup vinegar
1 teaspoon salt

Scrape and clean feet thoroughly. Boil with the pork slowly about 2 hours, adding water as needed; you should have a quart of broth after boiling. Discard the skin and mean parts. Add the seasoning, cut meat, and the gelatine previously dissolved in cold water; pour into cup or molds; when cold scrape fat off the top and serve cold.

49
Dutch Gravy

1 oz. of butter
2 tablespoons of flour
½ pt. of fish stock, chicken
    or veal broth
1½ teaspoons of lemon juice
    (for fish)

2 tablespoons white wine,
    for chicken
salt
2 yolks of eggs
¼ cup of cream

Melt the butter, stir in the flour, stew a few minutes, fill up with fish stock, stirring constantly. Season with salt and lemon juice (for fish), and add the 2 yolks of eggs.

For chicken or veal with rice, season with white wine. (This Dutch Gravy is indicated in this book for half a dozen other recipes as a sauce).

50
Dutch Horse-Radish Gravy

¾ cup cream or bouillon
1 pinch of salt
1 teaspoon of sugar

½ cup of horse radish
1½ teaspoons of flour
1 tablespoon of butter

Work quickly at scraping and grating. Stir in the horse radish, flour and butter and add the cream. Boil 15 to 20 minutes, stirring constantly, and season with salt and sugar. Serve with boiled beef, pot roast, etc.

51
Dutch Onion Gravy

1 small piece of butter	1 pinch of pepper
1 medium sized onion	1 tablespoon of vinegar
1 tablespoon of flour, salt	½ pt. bouillon

Brown the butter with the sliced onion; then stir in the flour, add the bouillon and season with salt, vinegar and pepper. Cook the gravy 10 minutes and strain through a fine sieve. Serve with boiled beef, pot roast, etc.

52
Dutch Fried Potatoes

6 potatoes	½ teaspoon pepper
3 onions	1 teaspoon salt

Boil the potatoes, unpared; remove skins when cold (or use left-over boiled potatoes). Fry the onions, sliced, with the potatoes, sliced, in covered frying pan for 15 minutes moderate heat, after seasoning with salt and pepper. Then uncover and fry hotly until golden brown.

53
Dutch Potato Croquettes

1½ cups cold mashed potatoes	¼ teaspoon salt
1 tablespoon butter	½ teaspoon minced onion
1 teaspoon minced parsley	Dash cayenne
2 tablespoons cream	1 egg

Mix into a paste the potatoes and butter, add the parsley, salt and pepper, cream, onion and egg (yolk only). Mold into croquettes, dip into the egg white, roll in cracker dust or bread crumbs. Fry in deep fat.

54
Dutch Pigs-in-Blankets

Slice or cut into dice ½ doz. potatoes, then boil soft. Take as many bread crumbs as potatoes, put crumbs into pan, with lump butter the size of walnut, parsley, salt and pepper to taste and a few slices of onion; fry until brown, then add potatoes. Make noodle dough, cut in squares, and put in filling as for dumplings. Drop these into the broth in which potatoes have been boiled.

55
Dutch Cheese Spread

1 cup cottage cheese	1 teaspoon salt
½ cup milk	½ teaspoon pepper
½ cup cream	¼ cup minced watercress

Put the cheese in a bowl, and pour in the milk and cream slowly, mixing with the back of a kitchen spoon. Bring to consistency of medium soft paste, adding the salt, pepper and watercress. Spread on bread (In olden days the Dutch put old-fashioned New Orleans molasses on top of this, on the bread.)

56
Ball Cheese, Millersville

1 gallon sour, thick milk

Let the milk get thoroughly thick and sour, then put into a cheesecloth bag and let the water drain from it. When drained salt it to taste. Form it into flat round balls about 3 inches in diameter, and lay upon china platters for three days. Then roll the balls in baking soda and wrap in paper. Place the balls in an earthen or glass crock and let ripen for two weeks. Then take them out and rinse in water to remove soda, scraping the balls with a knife. They are then ready to serve, to eat. They are good with rye bread.

57
Balla Kase, Womelsdorf

This is a rather strong and aged type of cheese. Thick milk is scalded lightly, the water drained off, and the curds preserved in a cold place in an earthen vessel, just as in making cup cheese. Once a week new curds are added, with a pinch of salt. Then the material is kneaded until smooth and sticky and shaped into balls. These are laid on a board to dry, and the temperature slowly raised for a day or so. Then the balls are placed in earthen pots and let stand for months. Sometimes such balls are made in the fall for use the next summer! The balls are washed and scraped to take off the mould outside, before eating. The longer they stand, the sharper the cheese.

58
Cup Cheese, Berks

This well known Dutch specialty, sold in all the farmer markets in the Dutch country, is made at its best in the following manner: Thick milk is scalded by placing a pan of it in the oven and baking the curd. Then the water is drained, the curds put in an earthen vessel and kept in a moderate temperature. Each day for a week new curds are added and mixed with the rest. Then the curds are poured into a heated pan and let simmer slowly and brought to a boil without stirring. Then a pinch of salt, a cup of cream, $\frac{1}{2}$ lb. of butter, and a teaspoon of baking soda are added, and the mixture is boiled for 15 minutes, with 2 or 3 beaten eggs added. Then the mixture is poured into cups and let cool.

59
Dutch Dandelion Wine

Gather (while the sun is shining) one gallon of dandelion blossoms. Pour over them 1 gallon of boiling water, then let stand in cool place for 3 days. Then put in a porcelain preserve kettle, add the rind of 3 oranges and one lemon, cut fine. **Boil** for 15 minutes and then strain. Add 3 lbs. of granulated sugar, together with the pulp and juices of the oranges and lemon. After it is lukewarm add one-half a yeast cake. Let stand for a week in a warm place and then strain again. Then let stand until it stops fermenting, after which bottle.

60
Pennsylvania Dutch Apple Butter

10 pounds apples	6 quarts cider
4 pounds sugar	2 tablespoons ground cloves
2 tablespoons ground all-spice	3 tablespoons ground cinnamon

Wash and quarter the apples. Boil the cider for 20 minutes then put the apples into the kettle with the cider and cook until **the** apples are very tender. Press through a sieve to remove skin and seeds. Add the sugar and spices to the pulp. Cook until as thick as desired (a soft paste) ; stirring frequently to prevent burning. Pour into crocks or glass jars.

4
Dutch Meat Dishes

Being their own butchers, in most instances, for several hundred years, the Dutch had every opportunity to make varied meat dishes. They never developed the "steak-chop complex" so common today, a complex which disdains to eat anything but steaks and chops. The Dutch, on the contrary, were the first in America to use the by-products of meat products with great ingenuity and skill. That is why Philadelphia Scrapple was born, and many sausages, aspics, etc. The Dutch cooked a wide variety of meat dishes and used all the techniques of appetizingly cooking the lesser cuts of meats, which every cookery expert knows to be the real test of a cook. The Dutch knew how to make meat products of the utmost savor and taste, and also how to cook it. True, a large number of the more illiterate and backward and poor subsisted monotonously on ham and a limited diet, but in all above-average households a remarkable variety of meat dishes were known and served—actually a wider variety than the household of today, with all its enlarged scope of foods available.

In meat pies the Dutch were also resourceful. These meat pies are described, however, in the chapter on Pies.

61

Liver Dumplings (Leber Kloese)

1 soup bone	½ loaf bread
1 lb. beef liver	2 eggs
4 onions	1 cup milk
	2 cups flour

To make stock for boiling dumplings, cook the soup bone in plenty of water for 2 to 3 hours, spicing it with salt, pepper, celery tops, parsley. Strain and keep hot while preparing dumplings. Scrape the liver, dice the onions and fry in butter. Season the milk and add the eggs, beaten, and make a soft paste with the flour. Shape into balls about 2 inches in diameter. Bring soup stock to boil, drop in dumplings, and boil without cover for 20 minutes. Serve on platter, and pour stock over it.

62

Dutch Spiced Pot Roast

Take a five or six pound piece of beef and spice with onion, bay leaf, cloves, vinegar, salt and pepper. It vinegar is too strong, add a little water. Leave the beef in the spice for 24 hours. Then brown on both sides, add the juice, and let boil 2 hours. Thicken with brown flour to make a good gravy. Put two tablespoons of butter on the beef when finished.

63

Dutch Baked Chicken

(*Quantity for 6 Persons*)

3 young, fresh chickens, salt	3 lbs. of lard for frying
⅛ lb. of flour	1 lemon for garnishing
2½ cups of bread crumbs	1-2 eggs

Preparation: The chickens are killed, dressed, washed, dried and prepared at once. Cut the chickens in half, salt them, dip them first into flour, then in beaten egg and then in bread crumbs. The lard is heated in an iron pot or kettle and the pieces of chicken placed into it carefully, one at a time, so as not to cool the fat too much and that the crumbs may not fall off. Bake them to a nice brown color. After the crust is hard, let them cook more slowly until well done. Then put on paper to drain, strew fine salt over the pieces and put on a platter after which they may be garnished with lemon slices.

64

Cornmeal Mush With Chicken

Chicken fricasee   Corn meal mush

Select meaty portions of chicken fricasee and gravy. Have cornmeal mush slices cut $\frac{1}{2}$ inch thick, dust with flour and fry golden brown. Serve chicken with mush slices and pour over gravy. (Rabbit is excellent used in place of chicken).

65

Goose-Liver in Jelly

$1\frac{1}{2}$ lbs. of fat goose liver
$\frac{1}{4}$ lb. of truffles
$\frac{1}{4}$ lb. of mushrooms
$\frac{3}{4}$ qt. very strong beef or chicken broth

$\frac{1}{2}$ teaspoon of meat extract
3 tablespoons of Madeira
10 pieces of white gelatine
1 white of egg and shell for clearing

Remove all fat from the broth, dissolve the gelatine in it, color with the meat extract, and season with Madeira. Add to it the white of egg beaten into some of the broth, and the crushed egg shell, toss over hot fire and set aside to clarify. Then strain through a fine cloth.

Skin in the goose liver and cut into $1\frac{1}{2}$ inch slices, also the truffles. Lard the liver slices with the truffles, then stew slowly in a little butter. When done, place them on absorbent paper to drain off the fat. Cook the mushrooms in bouillon for 10 minutes.

Into a dish set in crushed ice put part of the bouillon, let it

get stiff, and put in half of the goose liver, also half of the mushrooms. Pour more bouillon over this and cool, then repeat this
same process until all goose liver, mushrooms and broth have
been used. After it is stiff, turn out on a platter and serve with
a cold English mustard dressing, freshly made, and potato salad.

66
Dutch Chicken Floats

Remains of chicken meal	½ cup butter
1 cup mushrooms	3 eggs
2 tablespoons flour	1 teaspoon onion juice,
½ green pepper	lemon juice
2 cups cream	½ teaspoon paprika

Melt two tablespoons of the butter in a saucepan and fry the
green pepper (chopped and seeds removed). Then add the mushrooms (peeled and diced). Add the flour and cook until smooth,
but not brown. Then add the cream and cook until thick.
Pour in the chicken remains, boned and diced, and stand the
pan in hot water. Meanwhile beat the rest of the butter to a
cream, add the egg yolks one at a time while heating. Stir this
into the hot chicken mixture until the egg thickens, and cook
slowly. Add onion and lemon juice, salt, paprika. Serve on buttered slices of bread toasted on one side, the toasted side down.

67
Dutch Barbecue Chicken

1 broiler chicken	½ teaspoon onion juice
⅓ cup cider vinegar	½ teaspoon salt, pepper,
1 teaspoon kitchen bouquet	paprika, garlic
1 teaspoon Worcestershire	1 tablespoon tomato paste
sauce	½ cup melted butter

Cut the broiler in half down the back. Get the broiling pan
hot and grease well. Lay the chicken on rack and put immediately under hot fire. Sear on both sides. Have ready a barbecue
sauce made of all the other ingredients listed above. Have also

a new, clean paint brush, and during the broiling process paint the chicken on all sides at least three times with sauce. Make a gravy out of the drippings.

68
Dutch Liver-Oysters

1 lb. Calf's liver
2 eggs, beaten
½ cup bread crumbs

Place the liver in salted water and boil for 30 minutes. Then cut pieces about the size of an oyster, and dip in crumbs, then egg, then crumbs, and fry like oysters. Serve with lemon, and perhaps with squares of fried corn meal mush, or fried tomatoes.

69
Dutch Breaded Rabbit, Graul

2 rabbits
2 eggs, beaten
1 cup fine bread crumbs
1 tablespoon flour
1 cup milk or cream
Salt, pepper

Clean, wash, disjoint rabbit in several waters, and parboil for 10 minutes (water boiling when you put in the rabbit). Then take out and dip the pieces in beaten egg, then in bread crumbs; season with salt and pepper and fry in butter and lard, mixed, until brown. Then thicken the gravy with the flour and add the milk or cream and let come to a boil. Pour this over the rabbit, and add also onion sauce.

70
Kraut Chops, Christopher Dock
With Dutch Stewed Potatoes

6 or 8 pork chops
1 quart sauerkraut
2 tablespoons butter
4 or 5 potatoes
1 teaspoon minced parsley
1 onion
1 tablespoon flour

Cover the sauerkraut with water in stew pan and let simmer until tender. Keep warm while frying the pork chops. Then empty the drippings from the chops upon the kraut and let simmer for three or four minutes longer. Serve with the chops laid on top of the kraut.

Make the Dutch Stewed Potatoes as follows: Brown the butter, and mince the onion and brown it in the butter. Dice the potatoes, (which have been peeled and soaked in cold water overnight), put into the pan together with the parsley. Also 1 teaspoon salt, $\frac{1}{2}$ teaspoon pepper. Put in pan just enough water to cover and cook until tender. Then thicken with flour.

71
Spaetzle and Pot Roast, Zinzendorf

3 eggs	1 quart flour
$\frac{1}{4}$ teaspoon salt	Potroast

Prepare the potroast in the standard regular way as **always.** Make the Spaetzle to be served with it in the following manner: Mix the flour and salt in enough water to make a paste. Mold in the shape of thick noodle slabs, 3 inches long and a quarter of an inch or more thick. Boil them in salted water for ten minutes. Then take out and fry them in hot butter until brown. Pour over them the eggs, beaten, and fry again for three or four minutes. Sauerkraut is a good additional item for this meal.

72
Calf's Liver, Hiester

1 calf's liver	3 tablespoons butter
2 tablespoons catsup	1 tablespoon minced onion
1 tablespoon chopped green pepper	1 teaspoons Al Sauce (or Worcestershire Sauce)

Brown the onion in the melted butter. Pour in the sauce and catsup, add the pepper. Stir slightly and then pour over the liver in a baking dish. Add $\frac{3}{4}$ cup of water, and bake in a hot oven, basting occasionally.

73
Sausages, Barbara Frietchie

8 or 10 slices Lebanon bologna, or other large beef
   sausage

1 egg
$\frac{1}{4}$ cup dry bread crumbs
2 tablespoons butter

Dip the sausage slices into cold water and dry. Beat the egg, dip the sausage slices in it, and roll in the bread crumbs. Fry lightly on both sides in the butter. Serve with fried or scrambled egg, with water cress.

74
Hasenpfeffer, Berks

2 rabbits
2 onions
3 cups vinegar

1 teaspoon salt
$\frac{1}{2}$ teaspoon pepper
cloves, bay leaves

Disjoint and trim the rabbit, bone the meat and place in a Mason jar, and cover with the vinegar (with equal amount of water). Put in the jar also the onion and other ingredients. Let stand for 2 days. Then brown the meat in a frying pan in butter, turning frequently. Add gradually some of the liquid from the jar. Let simmer for 30 minutes. Serve with Dutch sour cream sauce.

75
Dutch Sausage and Gravy

2 lbs. Dutch pork or smoked
   beef sausages (or other
   sausages)
2 tablespoons butter or
   drippings

1 onion
1 cup bouillon or water
$\frac{1}{2}$ teaspoon meat extract
1 tablespoon flour

Fry the sausage over slow fire in the butter or drippings until brown; take out and put in the onion, sliced; add the flour. When brown, add the bouillon or water and meat extract. Cook for a few minutes. Pour gravy over sausage and serve, together with mashed potatoes and sauerkraut or cabbage.

76
Fried Dutch Sausages

2 lbs. Dutch pork or smoked beef sausages (or any other sausages)	1 cup bread crumbs
	$\frac{1}{2}$ cup flour
	1 tablespoon butter or
2 eggs	drippings

Salt the sausages, dip in a mixture of white of egg, flour and bread crumbs. Fry slowly to a nice brown crisp color. Serve with sauerkraut.

77
Pig's Knuckles and Sauerkraut Dumplings, Chester

1 qt. sauerkraut	1 teaspoon butter
6 pigs knuckles	1 teaspoon sugar
1 egg	$\frac{1}{4}$ teaspoon salt
Flour	

After washing the pig's knuckles in three waters, place in saucepan with sauerkraut and cold water and boil until tender. Then add the butter, melted, the salt, sugar and a half cup of water to the egg, well beaten, and flour enough to make a stiff batter. About 20 minutes before the sauerkraut and knuckles are finished cooking, drop spoonsful of the batter into the pot. Cover tightly and cook for 20 minutes.

78
Sauerkraut and Shpeck, Lehigh

2 lbs. fat shoulder of pork	mashed potatoes
1$\frac{1}{2}$ lbs. sauerkraut	

The sauerkraut is put into the pot on top of the pork and boiled until tender. Served with it are mashed potatoes, made with plenty of milk or cream mixed in.

79
Squab with Dumplings, Nazareth

3 squabs   Dumplings
2 teaspoons minced parsley

Split and stew the squabs with plenty of broth. Then make the dumplings, as indicated below, dropping the batter from a teaspoon into the boiling broth, adding the parsley, and covering tight and letting boil for 20 minutes.

Dumpling batter is made with 2 cups of flour, ½ teaspoon salt, 2 teaspoons baking powder, 2 eggs well beaten—mixed in milk enough to form stiff batter. When dropping batter into pot, push the batter from the spoon with a silver knife.

80
Chicken Jelly, Montgomery

2 cups diced chicken   1½ pints meat stock,
2 cups diced celery   seasoned hardboiled eggs,
2 tablespoons gelatin   pimento, green pepper

Dissolve the gelatin in cold water. Bring the soup stock to boiling point, add the gelatin, take from fire and stir until gelatin is well mixed. Strain. Immerse a mold in cold water and fill to depth of a quarter of an inch. Let chill, then arrange flat slices of hard-boiled egg, pimento, pepper, etc., and cover with another layer of gelatin. Repeat this process once more, and then mix the celery and chicken together and fill the mold. Pour over this the remaining gelatin and chill. Serve with lettuce and mayonnaise.

81
Poultry Stuffing a la Kraus

Giblets   1 apple, diced
1 onion   1 cup diced celery
½ cup pecan meats or   1 teaspoon minced parsley
    hickory nuts   1 teaspon salt
1 cup bread crumbs   1 teaspoon paprika
                                        1 tablespoon butter

Cook the giblets until tender, with the onion. Grind or mince them and mix with other ingredients. Double the portions for a large fowl.

82
Dutch Sauerkraut Partridge, Udree

Partridges
2 lbs. sauerkraut
1 cup peeled grapes

1 cup braised gooseliver
3 slices bacon

Roast the partridges, well buttered in the regular way; then bake in hot oven briefly in buttered casserole. Cook the sauerkraut, slightly with the peeled grapes and gooseliver. Place in casserole with partridge, covered with strip of bacon. Serve with sour cream sauce, and potato croquettes.

83
Partridge with Sauerkraut, Stiegel

2 young partridges
1½ lbs. of sauerkraut
2 tablespoons of butter
2 thin slices of bacon

1 wineglassful of white wine,
water for the sauerkraut
1 tablespoon of flour
1 apple

Singe, clean the partridge, dress and wipe. Tie bacon slices on, and fry for 15 minutes. 2 tablespoonfuls of butter. If the sauerkraut is too sour, soak it in water for a while, drain, then put it on the stove with the partridges and a little water, white wine, sliced apple. Cover and stew slowly for 2 hours. When the birds are tender, take off the bacon, stir a little flour into the sauerkraut; cook for a few minutes and serve hot.

84
Zitterling (Souse)

Scrape and wash 4 pig's feet. Cover with water and boil until the meat falls from the bones. Pick the meat from the bones, add 1 pint of the liquor in which the feet have been cooked, season with salt and pepper, and add vinegar to taste. Pour into a mold.

85
Beef Roll, "Rollardin"

Cut a round steak into pieces about 5 inches square. Cover each piece with thin slices of onion and bacon, dust with pepper and salt. Roll and tie each piece with string and potroast them for 2 hours.

86
Stuffed Beef Breast (Gefulte Rinderbrust)

1 beef fillet	$\frac{1}{2}$ lb. chopped meat
1 onion	$\frac{1}{2}$ teaspoon salt
1 teaspoon minced parsley	$\frac{1}{4}$ teaspoon pepper

Chop the onion, mince the parsley, add the salt and pepper. Spread this over the beef fillet, rub in well on both sides. Cover the fillet with the chopped meat, seasoned, and roll and tie it. Cook until tender in covered pot with one cup of water. Make a gravy to serve with it.

87
Baked Ham with Spiced Oranges, Kuechler's Roost

(As served at Kuechler's famous mountain restaurant near Reading, beloved of gourmets from far and wide while it existed.)

1 good smoked ham	4 oranges in shell
$\frac{1}{2}$ cup brown sugar	2 cups granulated sugar
1 tablespoon flour	$\frac{1}{4}$ cup wide cloves

Wash the ham in two waters, then bake in slow oven in two cups of water, until tender, allowing 21 minutes per pound. Then carve off the rind, and dot the ham with cloves. Then make a paste of the brown sugar and the flour and rub the ham with it. Bake for 20 minutes in medium oven. Serve with the following, (surrounding the ham on the platter) : Take four unpeeled Florida oranges and stick them with cloves; about seven to an orange. Then boil the oranges until the skin is very tender, in a syrup of two cups of sugar and two cups of water. Then cut the oranges in half, make a circle around the platter with them and pour some syrup over them. Serve all piping hot with stewed chestnuts (see index).

88

Sauerkraut and Brisket of Beef, Red Lion Inn

3 lbs. brisket of beef	1 tablespoon brown sugar
1 quart sauerkraut	1 tart apple, grated
2 tablespoons flour	1 small onion, minced
Salt, pepper	

In a large saucepan put one half of the sauerkraut. Sprinkle with flour, add the meat, onion, apple and sugar. Sprinkle with pepper and salt. Then lay the other half of the sauerkraut on top and cover with boiling water. Cover tightly and cook over slow fire for 1½ or 2 hours.

89

Sausages, Cornmeal Mush and Apples, Blue Mountain

Prepare and bake the mush (as described in Recipe No. 256). Then have some small pork sausages, sticking a fork clear through each one first. Put them in the frying pan, pour in boiling water enough to cover them and cook for 15 minutes. Drain out the water, and fry the sausages until golden brown, in bacon fat. After the sausages are finished, keep warm and fry the apples, peeled and cut into thin slices. Add more bacon fat or butter if necessary. Serve the mush, sausages and apples together, sprinkling a bit of sugar and cinnamon on the apples.

90

Hasenpfeffer, Col. Zimmerman

1 rabbit	½ cup celery root
¾ cup cream	1 onion
1 carrot	½ glass currant jelly
Flour	Vinegar
Salt, pepper	

Wash the rabbit in two waters, disjoint and soak in enough mild vinegar to cover, for six to eight hours. Drain, dry with a clean towel and rub well with pepper, salt and ginger. Then dip the rabbit pieces into flour and brown for 10 minutes in a frying pan. Then put into a sauce pan the carrot, celery root, onion and sufficient water almost to cover when the rabbit is added. Let simmer for 2½ hours. Take the rabbit pieces out and add the cream and the jelly. Stir well, and pour this over the rabbit. Serve very hot.

91
Ham and Pineapple, Shillington

1 good sized ham	1 cup pineapple juice
3 tablespoons flour	2 cups brown sugar
¼ cup cloves	2 cups pineapple rings

Wash the ham in two waters and boil it for an hour. Let cool in the water, drain, and then with a sharp knife remove the rind. Make a paste of 1 cup of brown sugar and flour, using some of the juice in the can of pineapple. Spread this paste over the entire ham to the depth of at least an inch. Now stick the cloves over the entire ham. Pour over it the remaining pineapple juice, and lay over the ham the pineapple rings. Bake in a slow oven for about 4½ hours (25 minutes to the pound). Baste frequently. Then make a paste of the other cup of brown sugar, using a little of the hot juice, and put over the ham thickly. Bake for 15 minutes more in still more moderate oven. Serve with the rings around the edges of the platter, and with some watercress.

92
Duck Mit Sauerkraut, Fritztown

Pick a young duck, and dress for roasting. Select a covered baking pan with space enough and lay the duck in the middle; put sauerkraut all around and on top, and pour in also the juice. Pour in also one cup of water. Stick in two small onions and sprinkle half a cup of sugar over the top. Put in a moderate oven and bake until tender. Serve with mashed potatoes made with plenty of milk.

93

Hasenkucha, Kuechler's Roost

Wash the rabbit in two waters, and disjoint. Soak in well-salted water for one hour (longer if an older rabbit). Wash in two waters again and parboil in salted water until quite tender. Then remove the meat from the bones and dice. Have ready Dutch stuffing (see index). Take a pudding dish or casserole and make successive layers, first of the stuffing, then of rabbit meat, then stuffing, pouring over each layer of rabbit meat a dressing made from the juice of the boiled rabbit thickened with some flour. Make three layers of both stuffing and rabbit, with rabbit on top. Bake brown in a quick oven.

94

Konigsberger Klops

1½ lbs. finely chopped raw beef	¼ lb. fat pork, chopped
⅛ lb. butter	1½ roll—the crust cut off
1 teaspoon minced onion	3 eggs
1 pinch of pepper	Salt
Juice of ¼ lemon	Some Flour

Mix the beef and pork well with the butter; soak a roll, press out and add together with other ingredients. Make small dumplings, rolled in flour, and boil slowly in bouillon or salt water for 15 or 20 minutes; or broil or fry them. Serve in deep dish with white fricassee gravy over them, add sauerkraut as a side dish.

95

Dutch Kidney Pudding

8 raw mutton kidneys	1 small onion
Salt	white pepper
2 tablespoons butter	juice of 1 lemon
1 tablespoon flour	18 mushrooms
½ cup rice	bouillon or water
1 tablespoon butter	2 egg yolks
½ pt. gravy or broth from meat	

Slice the kidneys ⅛ inch thick. Cook the butter, onions and sliced mushrooms; add flour, gravy, salt and pepper. Then put in the sliced kidneys and cook slowly 15 minutes. Add lemon juice.

Boil the rice until soft and mushy in bouillon or water, and then add the butter and finally stir in the 2 yolks of eggs. Butter a mold and sprinkle with crust crumbs; then put in a layer of rice and a layer of meat, alternately; the last layer rice. Cover and cook in a steamer over a kettle of boiling water for 2 hours. Serve on hot platter with Dutch gravy.

96

Spankerfel or Roast Little Pig, Spuhler

1 suckling pig	Salt
½ lb. butter	¾ pt. water
1 pinch pepper	

Wash and dress pig carefully, and soak in water for a few hours. Take out eyes and salt inside and outside. Bend the fore and hind legs under the pig and place in a pan on a rack. Pour in some water and let it roast for 10 minutes. Melt the butter, brush the pig with it every 6 or 7 minutes. Gradually add water and cook it 1½ hours. Prick the skin several times so it will not blister; the butter will make the pig crisp. The drippings can be served as gravy, or use tomato gravy.

97

Dutch Beef with Onions

1½ lbs. boiled beef	1 onion
2 tablespoons butter or suet	2 tablespoons flour
1 tablespoon vinegar	1 pinch of pepper
Salt	½ teaspoon meat extract
½ quart bouillon	

Mince the onion; simmer it in butter or suet until soft; add flour, simmer until brown. Pour on the bouillon, vinegar, salt, pepper and meat extract and let come to a boil. Cut meat in slices and serve hot in gravy.

98
Dutch Turkey Scallop

Dice left-over turkey. Make a layer of bread crumbs in the bottom of buttered baking dish; add then a layer of turkey, together with any cold dressing left over. Slice three or four hard boiled eggs, placing some with each layer of turkey.

Alternate the layers of meat and crumbs, adding bits of butter and seasoning to each. The last layer must be of crumbs. Place bits of butter over the top. Thin with milk any gravy that may be left, and pour over it. Cover the dish and bake 30 minutes. A few minutes before serving remove the cover and let the scallop brown.

99
Goose Stuffed with Apples

1 goose, 7 to 8 lbs.	1½ pts. water
Salt	6 pepper-corns
½ sliced onion	2 tablespoons flour
1¼ lbs. peeled, quartered apples	½ cup currants

Clean and dress the goose, cutting off wings, head, neck, feet. Trim off all fat, and soak this fat in cold water for 15 minutes. Rub goose with salt inside and outside. Mix the apples well with the currants and stuff into the goose, then sew up. Put the goose in the oven in a covered roasting pan with the water, sliced onion and pepper-corns, and roast for 1 hour. Remove the cover then start basting with the drippings every 10 to 15 minutes. If the water boils down, add spoonfuls of it so the fat will not get too brown. It may require from 2 to 3 hours roasting before the goose is well done and crisp. Sprinkle a tablespoonful of cold water over the skin to make it more crisp. Make gravy with flour. Skim off grease if too plentiful.

100

Pork Ribs and Sauerkraut, Balser Geehr

3 lbs. salted pork ribs	1 lb. sauerkraut
¼ lb. butter	½ teaspoon sugar
6 large peeled sliced apples	½ bottle white wine
¼ lb. chopped pork	¼ lb. chopped veal
1 egg	Salt
Pepper	1 tablespoon butter

¼ tablespoon minced onion

Salt the pork for several days then cut into pieces, wash, dry and fry on both sides in hot butter. Put into a pot with sauerkraut on top. (If the sauerkraut is too sour, soak it in water and drain). Add the quarter pound of butter, apples, white wine and sugar, cover and cook slowly for 2 hours. When it gets too dry, pour in some water. For the meat dumplings chop the pork and veal; add a soaked roll of bread, the egg, 1 tablespoonful of butter and onion, mixed. Shape into dumplings and fry well done in the butter in which the fried ribs have been. Serve the sauerkraut in the middle of the platter, the ribs around it and the dumplings piled on top in a heap.

101

Dutch Pork Pepper, Potts

2 lbs. lean pork	1½ tablespoons butter or lard
Salt	1½ tablespoons vinegar or 1
½ onion	wineglassful of red wine
1 bay leaf	Water or bouillon
3 tablespoons flour	Pepper
2 cloves	

½ cup pig's blood (can be omitted)

Dice the pork into 2½ inch squares. Brown the butter and flour, then add bouillon or water, onion slices, spices and salt, and cook for a few minutes. Put in the meat and cook slowly for 30 minutes. Add the vinegar or red wine and continue to cook slowly until done, about 45 to 60 minutes, or over an hour. Put the mixture in a warm dish and stir the blood into the gravy, strain and pour over the meat.

5
Dutch Ways with Eggs and Custards

No Dutch household outside of the cities was ever without chickens, and eggs were very extensively used.

The dish which apparently by consumer census is the most popular America dish with men (ham and eggs) is, of course, also very popular with the Dutch. Their ham is home-cured and immensely flavorful. It is usually cut too thick, to my point of view, but it certainly makes eggs thoroughly palatable!

The Dutch even *pickled* eggs; an art which one does not come upon often. And they have made an art of egg custards.

As for omelets (*Eierkuchen*), they have some interesting ones, a ham and bacon one (*Schnitzel Eierkuchen*) being rather special. A few Dutch also make a special favorite of mine (known also in New England), a Clam Omelette. There are also one or two other oddities.

102

Dutch Cheese Toast

Mix 4 tablespoonfuls of milk, ¼ teaspoon salt with 2 well beaten eggs. Dip four slices of bread into the mixture and fry a light brown on one side. Have ready 4 thin slices of cream cheese, slip one on each piece of bread as it is turned, cover, and by the time the under side of the bread is browned the cheese will be melted. Garnish with parsley and serve on hot plates.

103

Dutch Lemon Toast

Beat well the yolks of 6 eggs, and add 3 cups of sweet milk. Cut baker's bread, not too stale, into slices, dip them into the milk and lay slices in a pan with sufficient melted butter and lard to fry a nice brown. Beat the whites of 6 eggs to a froth, adding one cup of white sugar, the juice of 2 lemons and 2 cups of boiling water. Serve over the toast.

104

Dutch Coffee Custard

½ lb. roasted coffee   6 eggs
1 quart milk   6 oz. powdered sugar

Bring the milk to a boil, pour in the coffee freshly ground, cover tight and let stand for 30 minutes. Strain through a fine sieve.

Beat together the yolks of six and the whites of three eggs, and the powdered sugar, mix with the milk, strain once more, and pour into custard molds. Stand these in a pan of boiling water and place in a mild oven. Do not permit water to boil. When cooked stand away to cool off. Serve cold.

105

Dutch Apple Custard Pie

Take 1 pt. apple sauce, sweeten to taste, mix with it 2 eggs well beaten. Flavor with cinnamon and nutmeg. Bake in pastry.

106
Pumpkin Custard

½ pint pumpkin
2 eggs
1 tablespoonful flour
1 cup brown sugar

¼ teaspoonful ginger
¼ teaspoonful of nutmeg
1 lump of melted butter

Mix all with pint of milk and sprinkle cinnamon on top.

107
Pecan Custard

Grind ¼ lb. oi pecan meats very fine, warm 1½ pts. of milk with ½ cup of the pecan meats and 3 level tablespoonfuls of sugar. Remove from the fire and flavor with ½ teaspoonful of vanilla.

Let this stand if possible for 1 hour. Beat 4 eggs slightly and add to the milk and nuts. Season with ⅛ of a teaspoonful of salt. Bake in individual cups slowly for about 40 minutes. When turning these out sprinkle the remaining ground nut meats over the top of the custard.

108
Dutch Cup Cheese Breakfast Eggs

In the same frying pan in which you are frying eggs in butter, place slabs a quarter or a half inch thick of Dutch cup cheese—but select cup cheese which is not too pasty. It should have some coherence. Fry these slabs of cheese alongside the eggs, and do not try to keep eggs and cheese separate. Cut segments apart with knife as desired, and serve on hot plates.

109
Cornmeal Mush with Poached Egg, Otto

Cornmeal Mush
4 eggs

Cream sauce
½ cup canned corn

Poach eggs as usual. Fry cornmeal mush. Cut in ½ inch slices. Make a thin cream sauce and add ½ cup of corn, blending until smooth.

Arrange one poached egg on each slice of fried mush. Pour thin sauce around. Garnish with parsley. Serve very hot.

110
Breakfast, York

4 or 5 potatoes	2 teaspoons salt
2 eggs	5 tomatoes
2 tablespoons flour	½ teaspoon pepper
1 teaspoon minced onion	1½ lbs. smoked sausage
½ teaspoon baking powder	

The breakfast consists of potato pancakes, fried tomatoes with brown flour sauce, and the local smoked beef sausages (available anywhere in eastern Pennsylvania) or any sausages.

The potato pancakes are made by grating the potatoes—using about 3 cupfuls—after having peeled them and letting them soak overnight in cold water. Beat the eggs, add salt, pepper, flour and baking powder, then the onion. Mix well with potato. Drop batter on smoking hot griddle from a teaspoon, to make small cakes. Brown on both sides, serve hot with fried tomatoes and brown sauce made from the smoked beef sausage drippings.

111
Omelet Schnitzel

4 slices bacon	5 onions
½ slice ham	1 cup milk
4 eggs	5 slices bread

Dice the bacon and fry crisp, then fry the ham diced. Fry also the onions separately until brown, and then mix with bacon and ham in the pan. Beat the eggs, mix with milk and pour into the pan with the other ingredients. Cook for three minutes and keep stirring. Serve on slices of bread toasted on one side, (toasted side down).

112
Breakfast, Crefelder

Fry some cornmeal mush, and at the same time fry some tomato slices rolled in flour, and make a brown sauce. Fry also some eggs. Pour the sauce over all.

113
Kugelhopf, Lehigh

1 pint milk	1 lb. flour
½ lb. butter	1 yeast cake
8 eggs	1 tablespoon sugar
1 tablespoon minced citron	½ cup raisins

Mix the milk, butter and eggs in a pan and warm it. Add the flour and make a paste. Knead it, add the yeast cake, salt, and sugar, citron, and raisins.

Grease a mold, put in the mixture and let rise. Then bake in moderate oven for one hour.

114
Eggs, Dandelion

Prepare the dandelions (chopped fine) and dandelion sauce as elsewhere described (Recipe No. 202) and then pour it hot over poached eggs on toast (one side toasted served with the toasted side down on the plate.)

115
Eggs, Muhlenberg

Butter some pieces of dried beef and fry gently for a few moments. Serve with fried eggs and Dutch sauce.

116
Eggs, Smokehouse

Take some fresh or left-over ham and bacon together and dice it and fry lightly; also mince some water-cress or escarole or lettuce. Scramble some eggs, and fold in the ham, bacon and the greens.

117

Eggs, Sinking Spring

Fry the eggs in butter. Cut lamb kidneys or lamb's tongue, or both, into shreds about 2 inches long. Fry these (if possible in Port wine sauce) and serve with the eggs.

118

Oyster-Ham Floats, Perkasie

2 doz. oysters	1 tablespoon butter
6 slices boiled ham	1 teaspoon salt
1 teaspoon pepper	6 slices bread

Toast the bread slices on one side only. Lay toasted side down in bake pan, and place a piece of ham on each toast, and also four oysters. Sprinkle with pepper and salt and a piece of butter. Bake it in hot oven for 3 or 4 minutes (until oyster edges curl). Serve hot, with Dutch fried potatoes or Dutch Tomato Cakes.

119

Oyster Omelet, Delaware

1 doz. oysters	$\frac{1}{4}$ teaspoons onion juice
4 eggs	$\frac{1}{2}$ teaspoon minced parsley
2 tablespoons butter	$\frac{1}{2}$ teaspoon salt

Drain oysters and chop fine. Melt one half of the butter, add the parsley and onion juice and fry the oysters gently in this for 5 or 6 minutes. Beat the egg yolks, add the salt and the egg whites, stiffly beaten. Melt the other half of the butter, add the eggs, to the frying pan. When done, pour over it the oyster mixture and fold over. Serve hot with Dutch sauce or plain with watercress.

120

Corn Omelet, Althouse

¼ cup Shaker dried corn (or corn cut from cob)	1 tablespoon milk
4 eggs	¼ teaspoon paprika
1 teaspoon salt	1 tablespoon butter
	½ teaspoon pepper

After soaking the Shaker dried corn for about 12 hours in lukewarm water, or cutting corn from cob, simmer it in the butter in a frying pan, adding salt and pepper. Beat the eggs with the milk, add, and scramble in the pan. Serve sprinkled with paprika, and sprigs of watercress.

121

Omelet, Valley Forge

6 eggs	1 cup bread crumbs
1 cup milk	Salt, pepper, paprika

Boil the milk and pour hot over the breadcrumbs. In another dish stir the eggs, add the crumbs and milk, season with salt, pepper, paprika. Fry in butter and serve cut in quarters.

122

Dutch Springhouse Omelet

4 eggs	1 tablespoon butter
½ cup chopped watercress	½ teaspoon salt

Beat the egg whites stiff, add the salt, and stir in lightly the egg yolks. Mince the watercress (which so often grows in the springs by the "Springhouse" in Dutch country), and then melt the butter in the frying pan, cook the omelet 5 minutes. Fold in the watercress and serve.

123
Eggs, Lebanon

Eggs   Slices Lebanon bologna
1 tablespoon butter   (2 to each egg)
1 tablespoon flour

In a sizzling hot frying pan with the butter place slices of Lebanon bologna, cut about ¼ of an inch thick, and rolled in flour. Let brown for only a minute; break into the pan the eggs; one egg to each two pieces of bologna. Serve hot with watercress. (Lebanon bologna is a highly spiced home-made beef bologna sold throughout Eastern Pennsylvania and elsewhere. It can be purchased by mail from John Weaver, Lebanon, Pa.)

124
Fried Eggs, Conestoga

8 to 12 eggs   ¼ lb. ham
1 cup butter or good salad oil   1 teaspoon flour
6 ripe tomatoes   1 tablespoon butter
1 teaspoon sugar   ¼ onion

Slice the tomatoes and dice the ham. Melt the butter, stew the sliced onion and ham in it for 10 minutes, then stir in the flour, 1 pt. of water, tomatoes, salt, pepper, and sugar and cook 30 minutes. Then strain through a fine sieve, and sprinkle each egg with salt and pepper and fry in the butter, which should be very hot. Tip the pan or dish a little so the butter or oil covers the eggs. When the white of egg is firm, take it out and put it into a hot tomato dressing. Serve hot.

125
Dutch Egg Croquettes

Hard-boil 6 eggs. Cut in halves, remove yolk and mash these yolks with back of spoon. Add melted butter, salt, and pepper, and sweet cream enough to make a soft paste. Refill the white halves of eggs, and press together to form whole egg. Dip these whole eggs in beaten egg and cracker crumbs, drop in hot fat and fry a old grown. Serve garnished with lettuce.

6
Dutch Vegetable Dishes

THE VEGETABLE cuisine of the Dutch is based on the era before Texas, Florida and California out-of-season fresh vegetables; and also before the vogue of the tin can.

Consequently the Dutch had to be very clever and original with the few vegetables available in winter time, or even in summer time. Sauerkraut and cabbage were very heavily depended upon, and the changes rung upon these are very numerous indeed. But Spring had hardly arrived before the Dutch seized upon the dandelion to make one of their most delightful and original vegetable dishes. (See also dandelion "salads"). Most other people never get dandelion, or if they do, balk at them; largely because they are not picked before the plant flowers.

The Shaker dried corn is another original triumph which so many people knew nothing about. The Dutch also used chestnuts and Jerusalem artichokes more than most other people ever do. And in my opinion, the prize of all the Dutch vegetable dishes is Pod Peas, Mennonite — another item known to very few people.

126
Pod Peas, Mennonite

2 quarts tender English peas in pod
½ teaspoon pepper
2 teaspoonfuls salt
1 tablespoon butter

Wash and remove the stems of the youngest and tenderest English peas you can get. *But keep the peas in their pods.* Cook for an hour in boiling water to which the salt has been added. Then add the butter and pepper.

127
Dutch Baked Artichokes

10 Jerusalem artichokes
1 pt. soup stock
Salt, pepper, cayenne

Wash, but do not pare, and boil in a quart of salted water for 40 minutes. When soft, rinse in cold water and place in a covered casserole, pour in the stock, sprinkle with seasoning and bake 45 minutes in a hot oven, but uncover after 30 minutes.

128
Philadelphia Sherry Sauerkraut

2 lbs. sauerkraut
1 lb. bacon
2 apples
1 qt. soup stock
1 lb. German sausage
2 carrots
2 onions (stuck with cloves)
Parsley

Wash the sauerkraut in three waters, drain on colander. Place in stew pan with the bacon (parboiled), the sausage, carrots, onions, apples, parsley. Cover this with a piece of buttered brown paper cut to fit the pot, and pour over it the soup stock. Cook for 20 minutes, remove sausage and bacon and other things; put sauerkraut in a fresh stewpan and put it on the stove for one or two minutes, adding two tablespoons of the Dutch Sherry Sauce described in this book.

129

Dutch Cabbage

½ cabbage head
1 tablespoon butter
3 tablespoons vinegar
1 egg

½ cup flour
1 teaspoon brown sugar
½ teaspoon salt

Shred the cabbage, put in fat with half a cup of water, the butter, flour, sugar and salt. Stew for 20 minutes, covered. Add then the vinegar, and stir in one egg yolk beaten. Cover and let stand for an hour before serving.

130

Bean Schnitzel

1 slice bacon
1 tablespoon lard
4 onions
½ teaspoon red pepper

4 tomatoes
2 quarts string beans
1 teaspoon salt

Dice the bacon, fry it only a few minutes; add the lard. When melted and hot, the onions thinly sliced, also the tomatoes, chopped, and the string beans in one-inch lengths, put in salt and red pepper, simmer for 3 hours, adding one cup of water after one hour and stirring occasionally. Serve with the juices, reduced to sauce consistency.

131

Dried Corn, Shaker

1 cup Shaker dried corn
1 teaspoon sugar
¼ teaspoon paprika
1 teaspoon salt

1 tablespoon butter
¼ cup cream (or milk thickened with flour)

Shaker dried corn is a very delightful dish of great flavor, but it must be prepared carefully and slowly. It should be first washed, then simmered slowly for 5 hours, or else soaked in lukewarm water for 12 hours. If it is put on the stove in the morning to simmer in enough water to cover, add to it the salt and the sugar. If it boils dry, add water. It should simmer for at least 5 hours, after which add the butter and the cream (or milk thickened) with a teaspoon of flour mixed with water. Serve hot, sprinkled with paprika.

If left to soak 12 hours, it need not be simmered. Various recipes in this book call for Shaker dried corn, or suggest its use in place of corn from the cob or canned corn. Shaker dried corn can be obtained anywhere in Eastern Pennsylvania, or by mail from O. C. Stump, 13 West 23rd Street, Reading, Pa.

132

Cucumber and Bacon (Schmorr Gurken)

4 cucumbers	1 tablespoon sugar
3 slices bacon	1 tablespoon flour
2 tablespoons taragon vinegar	salt and pepper

Pare the cucumbers, and slice them thinly. Spread them in a bowl and sprinkle with a tablespoon of salt. Let stand for half an hour to draw their juice. Dice the bacon and fry them brown. Pour the bacon, with fat, upon the cucumbers. Put on the sugar and some pepper. Put them on the stove to simmer, covered, for 25 minutes. Sift the flour over them, and stir for three minutes. Serve hot.

133

Dutch Caraway Sauerkraut

1 pound sauerkraut (canned or fresh)	1 tablespoon lard
2 tablespoons caraway seed	1 potato

Bring two cups of water and the lard to boil. If the sauerkraut is very sour pour hot water over it in a colander. Put the sauerkraut in the boiling water, and add the caraway seeds.

If the sauerkraut is canned, cook one half hour. If fresh cook an hour and a half. Fifteen minutes before it is finished, look at it. If very juicy, add a grated raw potato, or a tablespoon of flour mixed with 2 tablespoons of water.

134
Dutch Red Wine Cabbage

1 red cabbage head	1 tablespoon butter
1 apple	1 wineglass red wine (or
¼ onion	half tumbler grape jelly)
1 tablespoon vinegar	

Bring to boil two cups of water in large pot; put in it a tablespoon of salt. Trim off three or four layers of the outer-leaves of the cabbage, and shred the cabbage. Rinse in two cold waters. Peel and core and cut into quarters the apple, and mince the onion. Put this and the cabbage into the boiling water, together with the butter and a teaspoon of pepper, and add the wine or jelly. Cover and let simmer gently for 55 minutes. Drain and serve.

135
Stewed Cucumbers

Pare and cut six cucumbers in quarters, lengthwise, removing the edge which contains the seeds. Soak ten minutes in cold water. Cook until tender in salted water. Make a thin white sauce with 1 cup hot milk stirred into 1 tablespoonful of butter and 1 of flour cooked together. Season with salt, black pepper, paprika and a bit of onion juice. Serve the cooked cucumbers on buttered toast and cover with the white sauce.

136
Stewed Chestnuts, Carl Schaich
(As served at Schaich's old-time restaurant near Reading)
Cook a pound of shelled chestnuts for two minutes in boil-ing water, and then remove the inner brown skin. Then cook

the chestnuts until tender *in beef broth,* into which is also put one teaspoon of chicken fat and a teaspoon of sugar. In a stew pan separately put one teaspoon of chicken fat or butter which has been browned, and a teaspoon of sugar. Dredge with a teaspoon of flour and cook until creamy and smooth, together with sufficient beef broth, and three drops of Parisian Essence. Then pour the sauce over the chestnuts in the pot and let stew for 3 minutes, adding a little more sauce and beef broth if necessary. The chestnuts are to remain whole and should be very soft and shiny. Now have ready one-half cup of large table raisins, which have been soaked in water for 2½ hours and then boiled soft. Mix these with the chestnuts and serve hot.

137
Cornmeal Mush, Schlatter

Cornmeal mush for frying is prepared as shown in Recipe Number 256.

Cut the slices into squares and diamonds and circles; then brush with milk and roll in very fine dry bread crumbs. Lay these pieces upon broiling rack, together with sausages, split open the long way. Broil these under moderately hot fire for 4 or 5 minutes and turn. Serve piping hot, sprinkled with water cress. Tomatoes if in season, sliced into half inch thick slices and broiled with the other things make an extra-fine combination.

138
Dutch Stuffing

1 egg	3 slices bread, cut in cubes
6 potatoes	1 green pepper, chopped
2⅓ tablespoons butter	2 teaspoons salt
1 onion, chopped	1 teaspoon pepper
1 stalk celery, diced	½ teaspoon paprika
1 tablespoon parsley	

Boil the potatoes in their skins, peel and mash. Then beat the egg and mix with the potatoes, together with salt and pepper.

Melt the butter and brown the onion in it, also the bread cubes. Then mix this together with the celery, parsley and pepper, and cook until tender, after which add the potatoes.

This stuffing is not only for any fowl, but may also be put into bread pans and browned in the oven and served with the fowl, or at any other time.

139
Dutch Fried Cucumbers

Pare and slice three cucumbers a quarter inch thick. Let soak in salt water for an hour, drain, wipe dry, and dip each slice into a beaten egg; then into grated bread crumbs. Fry brown in hot fat. Serve immediately.

140
Escalloped Beans and Corn

String and cut 2 quarts green beans. Cook until tender in salt water in which 2 tablespoonfuls of pork drippings had been added. Take 1 quart of green corn, cut from the cob, or Shaker dried corn which has been soaked in water for 12 hours, and cook 15 or 20 minutes. Put into a baking dish a layer of the beans, then a layer of corn, until the dish is full. Mix a cup of milk, two tablespoons of butter and 1 tablespoonful flour, pour into the dish, put into oven and bake 30 minutes.

141
Dutch Fried Chestnuts

1 lb. of chestnuts	1 pinch of salt
¼ lb. of butter	1 tablespoon of sugar

Shell and scald the chestnuts, and pull off the inner skin. Cook the chestnuts slightly in water, then put them into the butter, which has been browned and kept hot. Add salt and sugar and fry them light brown, shaking frequently. Serve with cabbage.

142

Sauerkraut Tulpehocken

4 lbs. fresh pork　　　　　　1½ cups barley
3 lbs. sauerkraut

Put the pork at the bottom of the pot (iron pots were the old-time method), and put the sauerkraut on top of it. Add enough water to just cover. Then pour in the barley, without mixing. Let simmer for 3 hours — do not stir. Then stir the pot and mix. Serve with boiled, mashed, or baked potatoes.

143

Dutch Baked Bananas

Use red bananas if you can get them. Wash them slightly, in cold water, but do not remove from skins. Cut a one-inch slit near the top end. Place in glass or earthen or enamel baking dish with 2 tablespoons of water for each banana. Bake in moderate oven for 45 minutes, until the skins are black. Serve in the skins, together with jellied water. Season with cinnamon.

144

Dutch Corn Floats

¼ lb. Shaker dried corn,　　4 slices bread toasted on one
　(or ¾ cup canned or fresh　　　side
　corn pulped or grated)　　1 teaspoon salt
1 tablespoon butter,　　　　½ teaspoon paprika
1 pimento　　　　　　　　2 cups grated American
½ cup tomato puree　　　　　cheese
2 eggs

Melt the cheese with the butter, then pulp or grate the corn and add. (Shaker dried corn must be soaked in water 12 hours in advance). Add also the pimento, and then the yolks only of the eggs beaten with the tomato puree, salt and paprika. Serve hot on the untoasted side of the toast slices.

145
Dutch Corn Hash

5 slices bacon
1 onion
1 can tomatoes

¼ lb. Shaker dried corn
(or 1 can canned corn, or
2 cups fresh corn)
paprika, pepper, salt

Dice the bacon and fry crisp. Mince the onion and add. When brown add the corn and then the tomatoes. Cook for 20 minutes, season. The Shaker corn must be soaked 12 hours in lukewarm water.

146
Dutch Baked Corn

¼ lb. Shaker dried corn
(or four ears fresh corn, or
1 can canned corn)
1 tablespoon butter
2 tablespoons flour

1 cup milk
2 eggs
2 teaspoons sugar
1 teaspoon salt, paprika
pepper

Melt the butter, mix with flour, pour milk in gradually, bring to boil. Add the corn (after pulping or grating) the seasoning and the yolks of the eggs well beaten. Then fold in the egg whites beaten stiff. Put in a buttered casserole and bake for 30 minutes in moderate oven. Serve hot.

147
Dutch Corn Onions

6 large white onions
2 eggs
¼ lb. Shaker dried corn
1 or 3 ears fresh corn
(or 1 can canned corn)

1 tablespoon thick cream
1 teaspoon melted butter
salt, paprika, sugar, Parmessan cheese, grated.

Parboil the onions and then remove the inside hearts. Pulp the corn (Shaker corn must be soaked 12 hours in lukewarm water in advance). Use only about 1 cup of the corn pulp, mixed with the eggs and the cream, the butter and seasoning. Fill the onion shells, sprinkle liberally with the Parmessan cheese and bake until the filling sets. Serve hot with a rich sauce.

148
Dutch Bacon Peas

2 lbs. fresh peas (or one can sifted peas)	3 slices bacon
1 teaspoon sugar	1 onion, salt, pepper

Add to the peas the sugar and the bacon diced (not fried), and the onion, diced. Cook until tender in limited amount of water. Let this water boil down pretty far.

149
Fried Potatoes, Siesholtzville

4 cups cold potatoes, diced	$\frac{1}{2}$ teaspoon pepper
3 eggs	2 tablespoons butter or
$\frac{1}{2}$ teaspoon celery seed	Crisco
1 teaspoon salt	

Melt the butter or Crisco until very hot, and then put in the potatoes. When they are nearly done break the eggs over them and stir quickly. Add pepper and salt and celery seed. Serve hot.

150
Dutch Fried Noodles

1 lb. egg noodles	3 tablespoons flour
6 or 8 slices bacon	3 hardboiled eggs
1 cup milk	$\frac{1}{2}$ teaspoon salt
2 tablespoons butter	$\frac{1}{4}$ teaspoon paprika
$\frac{1}{4}$ teaspoon pepper	

Home-made noodles are best, but good packaged noodles will do. Cook them in salted water until tender. Put in colander.

and let cold water run over them. Fry the bacon slices crisp and then put the noodles in the frying pan. In another pan melt the butter, adding the flour and the pepper, salt. Stir, and then add gradually also the milk, stirring until thick. Separate the hard-boiled egg whites, chop them and add them to this sauce. Serve the fried noodles on a platter, with the bacon slices around the edge, and then pour over the noodles the sauce. Rice the egg yolks and sprinkle them with paprika and spread on top.

151
Fried Potatoes, Leidy

After peeling and soaking potatoes in cold water for several hours, cut the potatoes into exceedingly thin slices, if possible with a slicer, so as to be almost paper-thin. Fry in bacon drippings to a golden brown, sprinkling caraway seed or celery seed over them. Bacon slices may be served with them.

152
Tomato Cakes, Kuechler's Roast
(To serve with Sausages, Kidneys, Sweetbreads)

These may be made from canned or fresh tomatoes, adding to 2 cups of tomatoes ¼ teaspoon sugar, ¼ teaspoon salt, 2 table-spoons catsup or chili sauce, dash of pepper. Sift ½ cup flour with ½ teaspoon baking powder, and add 1 tablespoon butter. Stir this into tomatoes, using flour just enough to make stiff batter. Fry on hot griddle greased with bacon drippings. Serve hot with broiled lamb kidneys, with brown flour gravy, or with sausages or sweetbreads.

153
Corn Fry, Hartranft

1 cup Shaker dried corn (or corn from 8 cobs)	2 tablespoons butter
	½ teaspoon salt
1 green pepper	¼ teaspoon pepper
½ cup milk	¼ teaspoon paprika

After soaking Shaker dried corn for 12 hours, in lukewarm water — or cutting corn from cob and also scraping the cobs, melt the butter in a frying pan and put in the corn and pepper (chopped), the salt and pepper. Cover and let cook gently for 3 minutes. Then add the milk, and let cook six or eight minutes. Sprinkle with paprika and serve hot.

154
Onions and Apples, Valley Forge

4 pieces bacon	4 onions
5 apples	

Fry the bacon crisp, place on hot platter. Then cut the apples, unpeeled into circles a half-inch thick. Parboil the onions, let cool. Then cut into circle slices. Fry the apples and onions together in the bacon fat (if not enough, add butter). Lift out on absorbent paper and serve with the bacon.

155
Lima Beans, Schwenkfelder

1 lb. lima beans	1 tablespoon butter
4 potatoes	$\frac{1}{2}$ teaspoon paprika
1 pt. milk	

Boil the beans, and when almost done add the potatoes, diced. When finished, drain and add the paprika, milk and butter. Serve hot.

156
Sauerkraut and Spaetzle, Beissell

2 eggs	1 lb. sauerkraut
Flour	$\frac{1}{2}$ teaspoon salt

Make spaetzle by mixing the eggs, half a cup of water, salt and enough flour to form very stiff batter. Roll out, lay on plate, and then holding the plate over a kettle of boiling water on the stove, cut the dough into odd sized pieces, like very heavy noodles. Skim out, drain, and season with bread-crumbs browned in melted butter.

Cook sauerkraut, and serve with spaetzle.

157
Dutch Succotash

½ cup Shaker dried corn
  (or 1 cup green corn
  from cob, or good
  canned corn)
1 pint green lima beans
1 pint stewed tomatoes, fresh

1½ cups potatoes
1 green pepper
2 onions
2 tablespoons butter or
  bacon fat
1 teaspoon sugar

In cooking pot melt the butter or fat and then put in the onions, minced, the green pepper, minced, the corn and lima beans. Cook for a minute, then add the potatoes, diced, and a quart of boiling water. Cook until tender, after which stir in the sugar, tomatoes, and 1½ teaspoons salt and ¼ teaspoon pepper. Serve with any of the dumplings described in this book.

158
Dutch Fried Green Tomatoes

6 large green tomatoes
1 egg
½ cup bread crumbs

1 teaspoon salt
1 tablespoon sugar
½ teaspoon pepper

Cut the tomatoes in slices one-half inch thick, and soak in cold salted water, for an hour. Then roll in the beaten egg and crumb mixture and fry in butter.

159
Dutch Corn Noodles

Soup bone (hip-bone with
  leg shank)
3 onions
4 potatoes
1 cup canned tomatoes
1 package bread noodles

3 teaspoons salt
2 tablespoons minced parsley
2 cups fresh corn, (or 1 can
  of corn, or ½ cup Shaker
  dried corn after soaking)

Cover the soup bone with water in a vessel with the onions
and salt, and bring to a boil, after which simmer for 3 hours.
Strain, remove fat; add to the boiling broth the noodles and
boil until tender. Drain, after which add the corn, the potatoes
(diced) the tomatoes and the parsley. Serve together on large
platter like spaghetti.

160
Fried Potatoes, Hanover

6 or 7 potatoes	1 tablespoon minced onion
2 tablespoons butter	1 tablespoon flour
1 cup soup stock (or cream)	1 teaspoon minced parsley
1 teaspoon pepper	1 teaspoon salt

Boil the potatoes, let cool. Dice and sprinkle with pepper.
Melt a tablespoon of butter, brown the onion in it; add the
flour and brown it, then add the soup stock or cream, and the
salt. Put in the potatoes and let absorb the sauce, letting boil
10 minutes. Melt a teaspoon of butter in a frying pan, add the
potatoes and fry until brown on one side, then turn. Sprinkle
with parsley and serve.

161
Grumbera Balla (Potato Balls), Lotz

8 potatoes	1 teaspoon minced parsley
1 onion	1 cup flour
2 teaspoons salt	1 cup browned breadcrumbs
$\frac{1}{2}$ teaspoon pepper	

Without peeling, boil the potatoes, and pare and grate
them when cold. Fry in butter, until brown, the onion, finely
chopped, add these to the potatoes, together with a beaten egg,
season with salt and pepper; make into the consistency of stiff
paste with flour. Mold into balls about $1\frac{1}{2}$ inches in diameter,
placing browned breadcrumbs and parsley in the centers. Bring
salted water to a boil, drop in the balls, cook uncovered for 20
minutes, until balls rise to top of water. Serve the balls cut in
half, sprinkled with browned bread crumbs.

162

Dutch Sauerkraut (In Quantity)

Put into large earthen jar a thick layer of cut cabbage, add ¼ cup of salt. Repeat until jar is filled. Put dry linen cloth over the top, add heavy weights (usually washed stones) ; let stand 2 weeks. Take off cloth, rinse, remove a little brine and replace cloth and weights; let stand again. This process requires about 6 weeks.

163

Dutch Welshkorn Oysters

1 pint of corn off cob (or well-soaked Shaker dried corn)	3 tablespoons flour
	1 teaspoon salt
	¼ teaspoon cayenne
4 eggs	¼ teaspoon black pepper

If using corn from cob, not only slice the kernels but scrape the pulp closely from cob. Add 2 beaten eggs and flour, pepper, salt, cayenne. Beat the yolks of two more eggs, then add well beaten whites, and flour enough to make stiff batter. Fry in butter in small pancake form; serve sizzling hot.

164

Dutch Bean Stew (Bohenenge müss)

1 lb. string beans	1 teaspoon butter
4 potatoes	1 teaspoon flour
1 tablespoon tarragon vinegar	Salt and pepper

Bring to boil two cups of salted water. Prepare the string beans, cut in half inch lengths. Boil them uncovered in the water, adding the butter. Peel and dice the potatoes, and add them to the beans after the beans have boiled for 15 minutes. Boil for 15 more minutes; then sift in the flour, sprinkle with pepper and add the vinegar.

7

Ways with Philadelphia Scrapple

Scrapple is the most nationally known of all Dutch foods. But very few—even of the Dutch themselves—have ever eaten scrapple in any other way than plain fried. It is of course delicious fried, but a few knowing Dutch cooks have learned to use scrapple more often, by treating it in a variety of ways.

Some of the ways are described in this chapter. Other combinations are possible, too.

165
Philadelphia Scrapple Croquettes

1 cup scrapple	$\frac{1}{2}$ cup cracker or
2 eggs hard boiled	bread crumbs
1 cup cooked rice	1 teaspoon minced parsley
or mashed potatoes	Salt, pepper
	1 egg, beaten

In a wooden or earthen bowl, mix well the scrapple, the rice or potatoes, the hard-boiled eggs, chopped fine. Season with parsley, etc., shape into croquettes with beaten egg and bread crumbs, fry in deep fat. Serve with horseradish sauce (see index), or with fried tomatoes.

166
Scrapple Cabbage, Bethlehem

½ lb. Philadelphia scrapple	1 cup fine bread crumbs
1 onion, chopped	1 cup milk
1 tablespoon cornstarch	1 egg, beaten
1 tablespoon chopped parsley	

Put the scrapple in a bowl and mix with the other ingredients, with a wooden spoon. Dress a well-formed head of cabbage and cut the top off neatly to make a "lid." Hollow out the center, to make a shell, with a hollow about 3 inches wide and 3 inches deep. Fill with the scrapple mixture and replace the "lid." Tie it in a cheese cloth and boil in salted water until tender. Such scrapple mixture as is left form into balls, dredge with flour and fry brown. Serve them on a platter around the cabbage. If desired make a tomato sauce to accompany it.

167
Baked Scrapple with Scalloped Potatoes

Butter a baking dish, and line it with sliced potatoes. Cover them with Dutch sauce or Horseradish sauce (see index). Mix a half pound of Philadelphia scrapple, together with a pinch of allspice and a cup of soup stock or leftover gravy. Heat this and then spread it over the potatoes. Bake slowly for 45 minutes until scrapple is brown and potatoes are cooked.

168
Scrapple Peppers, Germantown

1 egg	6 green peppers
½ lb. Philadelphia Scrapple	½ teaspoon paprika
1 onion chopped	1 teaspoon chopped parsley
1 cup fine bread crumbs	

Fry the scrapple lightly in slices, in butter, and then mix into a thick paste in a bowl with a wooden spoon, as well as possible, the scrapple, together with the drippings, the slightly beaten egg, onion, paprika, parsley and fine bread crumbs. Remove the ends and stems of the peppers and stuff them with the mixture. Lay them on their sides in a bake pan containing a little water and bake for 30 minutes, turning occasionally.

169

Scrapple with Pineapple Rings

1 lb. scrapple   1 can pineapple rings

Fry pineapple rings in butter on both sides until golden brown. Fry scrapple slices separately. Arrange on hot platter and garnish with pineapple slices.

170

Scrapple with Fried Tomatoes

1 lb. scrapple   flour, butter,
4-6 ripe tomatoes   salt, pepper

Cut tomatoes in halves, dust with flour, and fry in butter on both sides until soft and brown. Fry scrapples separately. Remove to hot platter and surround with fried tomatoes.

171

Scrapple with Fried Peppers

1 lb. scrapple   4-6 green peppers

Seed peppers and cut into thin strips lengthwise. Fry strips in butter until brown and soft. Fry scrapple separately, remove to hot platter and garnish with fried peppers.

172
Scrapple with Tomato Sauce

1 lb. scrapple
pinch thyme

1 can tomato soup or juice
$\frac{1}{2}$ teaspoon onion juice

Combine tomato sauce with thyme and onion juice and beat thoroughly. Cut scrapple into $\frac{1}{2}$ inch slices, dried in flour, and fry brown on both sides. Arrange slices on hot platter and pour over tomato sauce.

173
Scrapple with Spinach

1 lb. scrapple
2 lbs. spinach

Butter, salt, pepper

Cut scrapple in $\frac{1}{2}$ inch slices and fry on both sides to golden brown. Cook spinach, uncovered, drain and club lightly. Add. butter and seasoning. Arrange fried scrapple on platter and surround with well drained spinach.

8

The Dutch and Sea Food

Although a small portion of Dutch territory borders on Delaware Bay, the transport difficulties of olden days effectively kept a great plenty of sea food from most of the Dutch.

They are very fond of oysters, and throughout all Dutch cities and towns there has for a century or more been a great plenty of "oyster restaurants," the prime favorite being fried oysters, and next oyster stew, eaten with the familiar water-crackers which the Dutch prefer.

Cookery of sea food by the Dutch nevertheless developed some novelties. The tidy Dutch *hausfrau* has used the shad so common in the Delaware, and early learned to bone them and also to *plank* them. The Dutch in Philadelphia, Chester and other near-shore places developed some very good sea food recipes, while at a few gourmet restaurants on the Reading hills a few particularly fine recipes were used.

174

Baked Lobster, Frank Lauer

(As served at Frank Lauer's famous hillside place near Reading —now only a memory)

Have your lobsters split and the claws cracked. Use a large roasting pan and arrange the lobsters in them. Sprinkle with paprika and lay a piece of butter on top of each piece. Put in extra hot oven. Baste every few minutes with a sauce made of melted butter which has been boiled with one finely chopped clove of garlic and ½ teaspoon finely chopped parsley. Let bake for 20 minutes. Serve sizzling hot, sprinkled with paprika; but first mix the green stuff from the lobster heads with the juice collected in the pan and the remainder of the melted butter, and bring to a boil. Serve this sauce separately with the lobster, together with sliced tomatoes, and baked potatoes (or Dutch chow-chow, pretzels and beer).

175

Fish Macaroni

½ lb. of macaroni	1 tablespoon of flour
3 qts. of water	1 pt. of cream or milk
1 tablespoon of salt	2 tablespoons of lemon juice,
2 lbs. of boiled fish	salt to taste
¼ lb. of grated Parmesan	1 pinch of pepper
cheese	½ cup sliced mushrooms
½ pt. of white wine	¼ lb. of butter

Boil the macaroni in salt water after breaking into inch-long pieces. Clean the fish, dress and boil in salt water. Take out the skin and bones and cut the fish into small pieces. Butter a baking-dish, fill with a layer of macaroni, then fish and Parmesan cheese and mushrooms. Sprinkle with white wine; repeat this 3 times, but have the last layer macaroni. Make dressing of ¼ lb. of melted butter into which the flour, cream or milk, lemon juice, salt and pepper are stirred. Pour over the macaroni, the ⅛ lb. of butter cut in small pieces, sprinkled over the top and bake in moderate oven.

176
Dutch Baked Pike

Pike
4 tablespoons butter
2 onions
1 teaspoon flour
1 tablespoon sweet cream
1 teaspoon sugar

1½ cups sour cream, paprika,
 salt
2 tablespoons grated
 Parmesan cheese
2 tablespoons cracker dust

Cut the pike down the middle, removing bones but leaving the skin as whole as possible. Wash in two waters and dry. Rub with salt, inside and out; place in roasting pan, cover well with butter, and bake for 8 minutes. Then place over the fish the onions, minced, after stewing them light brown in butter, with paprika and sugar.

Add also the sour cream, together with the flour which has been made into a paste with the sweet cream. Bake 10 minutes, and baste frequently; also sprinkle over it the cheese and the cracker dust, and then bake 10 minutes until light brown. Serve hot, with the sauce, and lettuce leaves, carrying also dabs of horseradish.

177
Dutch Walnut Shad

(Also applicable to sea bass, pike, whitefish, lake trout)

½ lb. shelled walnuts
2 tablespoons flour
1 teaspoon sugar, shad
2 onions

1 carrot
1 leek, celery leaves
½ teaspoon minced parsley
½ clove garlic

Boil for 45 minutes water in which is placed the onions, carrot, leek, knob-celery or celery leaves, parsley, 4 cloves garlic cut small; the carrot cut in thin slices. Have the shad cleaned and rubbed with salt, let stand for an hour, cut into pieces 1½ inches wide. Place in the boiling water, (just enough to cover) and only simmer it for 10 minutes. Then let cool in water.

Make walnut sauce by grinding quite fine the walnuts, and

mix into a smooth paste with 2 tablespoons flour, cold water, one half clove, and crushed garlic. Then add ½ teaspoon black pepper; the sugar and enough of the fish water to make into sauce consistency, and cook for 30 minutes, until creamy but not thick.

Serve the fish on platter with both head and tail, lay some carrot slices on it and pour plenty of sauce over it; garnish with lettuce leaf and horseradish.

178
Oyster Pot Pie, Allentown

1 quart oysters	1 teaspoon paprika
2 tablespoons butter	1 teaspoon minced parsley
1 tablespoon flour, or more	Biscuit

Scald the oysters in their own liquor; when the water boils skim out the oysters and keep warm. Add to the oyster liquor a pint of water, a teaspoon of salt and half a teaspoon of pepper and the parsley. Also the butter. Thicken with the flour, mixed with a little cold water. Have ready some light biscuit dough, which cut into squares and drop into the hot oyster liquor. Cover tight and cook for 20 minutes. Then stir the oysters in and serve in one dish, sprinkled with paprika.

179
Philadelphia Fried Oysters

50 prime oysters	Cracker or fine dry
2 eggs beaten	bread crumbs
Mayonnaise dressing	salt, pepper

Make a batter of the eggs, well beaten, seasoned with salt and pepper, and using some of the strained liquor of the oysters. Pick the oysters out of the liquor and roll in the crumbs, then in fresh mayonnaise; then in batter; then again in crumbs. Pat them with your hand to firm the crumbs. Lay upon a platter, and fry in hot fat. Serve at once with catsup or lemon slices, and Dutch butter pretzels or water crackers.

180
Dutch Cod Fish Balls, Clam Dressing

1 quart mashed potatoes	1 egg, beaten
1 pint salt cod fish	1 tablespoon butter
¼ teaspoon red pepper	½ cup cracker crumbs
1 teaspoon black pepper	Dressing: 10 clams, ⅛ lb. but-
1 teaspoon minced parsley	ter, 1 pint milk, 1 tea-
2 onions, chopped	spoon minced parsley

Boil the salt cod, after soaking in water; shred and mix with the potatoes, peppers and salt, onion and parsley, butter. Make into balls; dip in the beaten egg and cracker crumbs, and fry to golden brown in butter or Crisco. Drain, and serve with a clam dressing, made as follows: Mix one eighth of a pound of butter, browned, and 10 chopped clams, plus a little salt and pepper, a pint of milk and a teaspoon of chopped parsley. Bring to a boil and pour over the codfish balls just before serving.

181
Dutch Broiled Salt Mackerel

2 or 3 salt mackerel	1 teaspoon salt
3 tablespoons butter	½ teaspoon pepper

Place the salt mackerel in a pan of water, skin side up, for 24 hours, changing the water 3 times. Wipe dry, and then broil on both sides, the skin side last. Season with salt and pepper, and serve hot, with the butter melted on top of it, and perhaps some fried corn meal mush squares with it, or broiled or fried tomatoes, or both.

182
Dutch Spiced Shad

2 Delaware shad	pepper, 1 or 2 bay leaves
2 or 3 cups cider vinegar	1 onion, sliced
sugar, cloves, allspice, salt,	3 red peppers

Split the shad along the backbone, remove bone, then cut

into pieces about an inch long. Put these pieces into an earthen crock, in layers: first a layer of fish, then sprinkle with salt and pepper, a few cloves, allspice and a whole pepper, some onion slices and one or two bay leaves. Repeat with another layer of fish until used up. Dilute the cider vinegar with one half the quantity of water, adding a few teaspoons of sugar. Pour this over the fish. Lay a plate over the crock and put in a slow oven for 2 or 3 hours, until the fish is tender. Stand out to cool, and serve the next day with lettuce.

183
Corn Fish Cakes, Royersford

1 cup shredded fish	1 tablespoon minced parsley
2 cups corn meal mush	$\frac{1}{2}$ teaspoon salt
2 tablespoons chopped onions	

Put all the ingredients in bowl and mix with a wooden spoon. Shape into cakes and brown them in a pan in the oven. Serve with tomato sauce.

184
Oysters, Ontelaunee

2 dozen oysters	12 slices bacon
1 pan cornmeal mush	12 teaspoons catsup

Fry the bacon crisp, place on hot plate, and then fry the oysters in the bacon fat for just a few minutes until their edges curl. Then carefully cut 12 slices of corn meal mush each about $\frac{3}{4}$ inch thick, slicing a pocket in the middle of each piece, into which insert two oysters and a slice of bacon, also a teaspoon of catsup. Squeeze shut the pocket. Fry these slices in the bacon fat until a light brown. Serve very hot with watercress.

185
Fried Oysters, Harbaugh

2 dozen oysters	1 green pepper
2 eggs	$\frac{1}{2}$ cup minced ham
1 cup dry bread crumbs	

Wash and drain the oysters, and roll them twice alternately in the eggs, beaten, and then the bread crumbs which have been mixed with the pepper and ham, both very finely minced. Fry in butter. The bread should be very dry before crumbing, and should be crumbed very fine.

186
Dutch Oyster Peppers

4 large green peppers	3 tablespoons butter
$\frac{1}{4}$ teaspoon baking soda	$3\frac{1}{2}$ tablespoons flour
1 cup browned bread crumbs	$1\frac{1}{2}$ cups milk
1 quart oysters	$\frac{3}{4}$ teaspoon pepper, salt

Wash and wipe dry the peppers, and parboil for 10 minutes in 1 quart water, with the baking soda. Cut in half, remove seeds, and fill with a mixture of the oysters and the cream sauce. Sprinkle generously with the bread crumbs. The oysters should first have been washed and cooked gently until plump. The cream sauce is made by mixing the butter, flour, milk, salt, and pepper.

187
Macaroni and Oysters

Put 2 cups elbow macaroni in boiling water, boil rapidly for twenty minutes. Drain and dry twenty-five oysters, put a layer of macaroni in the bottom of a baking dish, then a layer of oysters, sprinkling them with salt and pepper, and so alternately until used up. Cover with bread crumbs, dabbing the top with a few bits of butter and brown in oven for twenty minutes. Then add strained oyster liquor to moisten, and a cup of milk.

188
Broiled Oysters with Brown Sauce

Large oysters only should be used. Drain them, and keep one pint of liquor to every twenty-five oysters. Boil the liquor, skim off the surface. Put one tablespoonful of butter in a frying-pan and stir until it is a nice brown, then add two tablespoonfuls of flour, mix well, and brown. The oyster liquor should now be added. Stir constantly until it boils.

Season with salt and pepper, pour into a porcelain-enamel sauce-pan and stand it over hot water until wanted. Wipe the oysters with cloth, lay them on a clean towel, and shake salt on them.

Put the oysters on a very hot griddle, and turn them when brown. When browned put them into the brown sauce. Serve on buttered toast.

189
Dutch Chicken Oyster Pie

Stew chicken until tender, season with quarter pound butter, salt, and pepper. Line deep pie dish with pastry crust. Pour in the stewed chicken and cover loosely with a crust, cutting in the center of this crust a hole the size of a small teacup. Prepare separately one pint of oysters, heating the liquor, thickening with a little flour and water. Season with salt, pepper, and two table-spoons of butter. When it comes to a boil, pour over the oysters. Twenty minutes before the pie is done, lift the top crust and put the oyster mixture in.

190
Shrimp Wiggle, Esche Puddle

One large can of shrimp, one can of small peas, one-half pint cream, one tablespoonful flour, 2 tablespoons butter, seasoning.

Cut shrimp into small bits and let stand in a flat dish for an hour. Drain peas and also let stand. Mix a sauce of cream, but-ter, and flour, into this put the shrimp and the peas. Heat very slowly, stirring constantly to avoid scorching. Season to taste.

191
Fish in Jelly

2½ lbs. of fish
2½ qts. of water, salt
4 peppercorns
2 cloves
2 lemon slices

2 tablespoons of vinegar
4 tablespoons of lemon juice
½ cup of white wine
10 pieces of white gelatine
1 bay-leaf

Boil all the ingredients, then put in the fish, dressed and cleaned. Let simmer gently for 30 minutes. Take out the fish, remove the bones and cut it up into large pieces. Boil the fish stock down to 1¼ qts. Dissolve the gelatine in it, then boil for one hour, strain and pour on the fish to cool. Garnish with lettuce.

192
Oyster and Caviar in Jelly

1 qt. strong beef bouillon
3 tablespoons of white wine
1 tablespoon of lemon juice
2 whites of eggs and shells

4 doz. oysters
12 layers of gelatine
¼ lb. of caviar, ice

Skim carefully from the beef bouillon, season with white wine and lemon juice, and dissolve the gelatine in it. Stir the white of egg with some bouillon and add it, put in the crushed egg shells to cook for a second, then set aside to clarify. Strain it through a fine cloth. Open the oysters, clean and cut out of the shells. Place dish on chopped ice, place some oysters in a circle into the dish, with sufficient cold bouillon to cover; let get stiff. Repeat until all oysters have been used. Put the rest of the bouillon on top and let get stiff.

Pour the caviar into a sieve, let very cold water run over it until it becomes granular. In the center of the oyster jelly cut out a round hole, just large enough to hold the caviar. Heat the oyster jelly that has been cut out and pour it over the caviar. When it is perfectly stiff, turn it out on a platter and garnish with lemon slices and lettuce leaves. Serve with a cold English mustard dressing, freshly made.

193
Dutch Baked Eel, White Horse Inn

3½ lbs. of eel, salt
1 beaten egg, flour for
   dredging

1 pinch of pepper
¼ lb. of butter or lard for
   frying

Skin and clean the eel, cut into three inch pieces, and bone. Rub with salt and pepper, roll in beaten egg and flour, and bake in hot butter to a nice brown color. Serve Dutch Dressing with it.

194
Dutch Beer Eel, Frank Lauer

3½ lbs. of eel
3 tablespoons of butter
2 tablespoons of flour
1 qt. of light beer
½ onion, sliced

¼ lemon, sliced,
1 pinch of pepper
1 clove
½ bay-leaf
salt

Have the eel skinned and cleaned and cut into three inch pieces, and remove the bones from the pieces. Stir the 3 tablespoonfuls of butter into the flour, add the beer, also all the spices, lemon and onion slices. Cook this gravy and put in the pieces of eel to boil 20 minutes. Serve the eel on a hot platter, strain the gravy, thicken it with flour and boil, and pour it over the eel.

195
Oyster Bake, Frank Lauer

6 slices bacon
1 tablespoon minced parsley

24 large fat oysters
1 teaspoon onion juice

Fry bacon for 2 or 3 minutes. Sprinkle a bit of onion juice on them and a bit of parsley. Then put the oysters in a pan in their own liquor and stew them for just one minute. Then lift out, dry them on clean towel, and roll each oyster in one of the pieces of bacon and then fasten with a wooden tooth-pick. Sprinkle bacon with paprika. Then put them in a roasting pan and bake in a hot oven for five or six minutes. Serve on Pilot crackers two oysters to each cracker, and pour over it Horse-radish sauce (see index).

196
Fish Fillet, Philadelphia

3⅓ lbs. fish	4 pepper-corns
Salt	1 bay-leaf
Juice of 1 lemon	½ onion
¼ lb. butter	Skin
Pepper	2 cloves
Bones	2 slices of lemon
1½ qts. water	

Bone the fish and cut into equal fillets. Salt and let stand for 30 minutes. Prepare the fish bouillon, bringing to boil the bones and skin in 1½ qts. of water to which the pepper-corns, cloves, lemon and onion slices and salt have been added. Cook until the water has boiled down to ¾ qt. Then put the fish fillets into a buttered pan, season with 1 pinch of pepper, lemon juice; place the ¼ lb. of butter in pieces on top. Pour ½ cupful of the fish bouillon over them.

Cover the pan, stew in the oven for 25 minutes. Serve on a hot platter, pouring the drippings over with Dutch Gravy.

9

Dutch Salads

The Pennsylvania Dutch, like most people of long ago, ate too few greens. Their salads in the modern sense of greens, fruits and vegetables, are therefore not notable.

But some of their salads and salad dressings are very notable. Thus their hot salad dressing is a tremendously tasty thing; and used on dandelions or watercress, I think it is a triumph of gastronomic delight, one of the outstanding Dutch dishes. So, too, is their Hot Potato Salad. Their sour cream dressings are also most delicious. Elsie Singmaster, novelist of the Pennsylvania Dutch, selected one of these for me as her favorite Dutch recipe. Their bean salad is also delicious.

197
Sour Cream Salad Dressing, Singmaster
(Favorite Dutch recipe of Elsie Singmaster, novelist)

½ pint thick sour cream   chopped chives or
2 tablespoons white vinegar   onions

Mix the above ingredients freshly, and add sugar, salt and pepper to taste. Serve on sliced cucumbers, young lettuce or cabbage.

198
Dutch Dandelion and Lettuce Salad

1 lb. young dandelions   ½ green pepper
1 head iceberg lettuce   2 hard boiled eggs
4 onions   ¼ lb. Swiss Cheese
2 tomatoes   ¼ teaspoon cayenne pepper
2 teaspoons salt   ½ teaspoon pepper
3 tablespoons olive oil   4 tablespoons vinegar

Select dandelions if possible from stalks which have not flowered. Chop the dendelions and lettuce and pepper. Cut the cheese into very small pieces. Mix thoroughly in a bowl with the cayenne and salt and pepper, and then the oil and vinegar. Then the tomatoes, diced, and the eggs, diced, stirring lightly so as not to smash tomato and eggs.

199
Dutch Hot Potato Salad

10 Potatoes   2 tablespoons vinegar
1 onion   ½ teaspoon salt
2 slices bacon

Boil potatoes in skin, which remove when cold. Dice or slice them, add sliced onion. Then dice the bacon and fry the pieces crisp. Add the vinegar and salt. Pour this over the potato, mix, and serve hot.

200
Dandelion Salad, Wissahickon

2 eggs	1 tablespoon sugar
5 slices bacon	1 teaspoon salt
½ cup cream	2 tablespoons butter
4 tablespoons vinegar	¼ teaspoon paprika
1 lb. young dandelions	½ teaspoon pepper

Wash and dry dandelions (preferably picked from stalks which have no flowers), place in salad bowl and let stand in warm place. Dice and fry the bacon, and then drop the bacon pieces and the fat on top of the dandelions. Mix the butter and cream and melt slowly; beat the eggs, add pepper and salt, vinegar and sugar and mix with the warm cream mixture. Pour into the fry pan and stir until it thickens like a custard. Pour this smoking hot over the dandelions and stir well.

201
Hot Potato Salad, Perkiomen

4 potatoes	1 teaspoon sugar
3 eggs	1 teaspoon celery seed
1 cup vinegar	salt, pepper
1 cucumber	1 onion

Boil the potatoes, let cool, pare and dice; beat the yolks of the eggs, add salt and pepper and sugar and celery seed. Put on fire and stir until it comes to a boil. Then let cool. Dice the onion and cucumber and add, then pour on the vinegar.

202
Dandelions, Schuylkill

1 quart young dandelions	1 teaspoon butter
1 cup sour cream	2 teaspoons sugar
1 egg	1 tablespoon vinegar

Wash dandelions carefully, cut off some of the ends of the older leaves. Make a mixture of the sour cream, well-beaten egg, salt, butter and the sugar (dissolved in the vinegar). Let come to a boil in stew pan, then put in the dandelions.

203

Jerusalem Chicken Salad

2 cups diced Jerusalem
    artichokes, cooked
2 cups diced chicken

¼ cup French dressing
½ cup sliced radishes
Mayonnaise, lettuce

Cook the artichokes in salted water for 40 minutes, cool and dice. Combine with the radishes, then with the chicken and French dressing; serve with lettuce and mayonnaise.

204

Corn Salad, Amish

1 doz. ears of corn, or
    1½ cups Shaker dried
    corn
1 head cabbage
5 sweet peppers

2 teaspoons mustard (prefer-
    ably English mixed with
    a little of the vinegar)
1 pint vinegar
1 teaspoon salt
1½ cups sugar

Chop the peppers and cabbage. (If using Shaker dried corn soak in lukewarm water for 12 hours.) If using fresh corn, cut from the cob. Mix all ingredients, add a pint of water and cook for 15 minutes. Serve hot, or cold with lettuce or cress.

205

Dandelion Salad, Mifflin

1 lb. young dandelions
3 slices lean bacon
2 eggs (yolks only)
1 tablespoon sugar
½ pint sour cream

½ teaspoon salt
¼ teaspoon pepper
½ teaspoon Colman's
    English Mustard
1 teaspoon flour
2 tablespoons vinegar

Dice the bacon and fry crisps. Mix the other ingredients (dissolving the dry mustard in a little of the vinegar), and add to the bacon in the pan. Stir constantly, and when it starts to boil add quickly the well-cleaned dandelions, which do not scald. Serve hot with sliced hard-boiled eggs.

206
Dutch Salad Cream

1 cup butter	1 cup thin cream
½ cup vinegar	½ teaspoon salt
6 egg yolks	sprinkling of cayenne and white pepper

Boil together in deep, porcelain enamel saucepan, the vinegar, and butter. Beat the egg yolks lightly, and pour over gradually the boiling vinegar and butter, beating the mixture meanwhile. Put on fire and beat rapidly while on the fire until it begins to thicken (taking care not to scorch). Then gradually pour in the cream. It should not be brought to the boiling point. Add salt and pepper, take off fire and beat it in a pan of cold water until cool.

207
Dutch Bean Salat

2 lbs. yellow string beans	1 onion
1 tablespoon butter	1 teaspoon salt
3 cups vinegar	

String the beans, wash in several cold waters. Into a kettle of boiling water, add the butter, then slowly the beans, which cook until tender. Let cool, add the onion, chopped. Put in vinegar, and let stand *for two days*. Drain off the vinegar, boil it, adding a little water if it is too sour. Pour this hot over the beans. Pack the beans in glass jars, pour in the vinegar almost to top, filling the rest of the space with good olive oil. Screw on caps and keep in cool place. Serve with lettuce or in relish dishes.

208
Dutch Hot Salad Dressing

3 slices bacon	1 egg
3 tablespoons vinegar	1 tablespoon sour cream
1 teaspoon flour	½ teaspoon pepper
½ teaspoon salt	

Dice the bacon and fry crisp. Add the vinegar and sour cream, also the flour made into a paste with a little water, and the yolk of one egg.

209
Dutch Cucumber Salad

1 teaspoon salt	1 pint sour cream
1 onion	2 cucumbers
2 tablespoons terragon vinegar	½ teaspoon pepper

Slice the cucumbers as well as the onion, sprinkle with **salt**. Let stand a half hour, place in cheese cloth and squeeze out water. Place the cucumber mixture in dish, add the vinegar, **and** mix. Pour the sour cream over it, and sprinkle with pepper.

210
Dutch Hot Slaw

Shred small head of cabbage, put into pan with cabbage, together with two tablespoons of butter, and steam until soft. Beat 1 egg, ½ cup vinegar together, pour over cabbage, salt and pepper to taste. Serve hot.

211
Dutch Chestnut Salad

Blanche 1 pint of shelled chestnuts, and boil slowly in salted water until tender. Drain and allow to cool. To the chestnuts add an equal quantity of celery cut fine. Mix with a mild mayonnaise dressing (or Dutch Sauce) and serve on lettuce leaves.

212
Hot Endive Salad

Cut a good sized head of endive into about 2 inch lengths. Put 2 tablespoons of vegetable shortening or lard in a skillet and let it get thoroughly hot. Stir the endive, seasoned with a little salt, in this; add a little water and stand back on the stove to simmer for about half an hour. Make a dressing of vinegar, sugar, and water, and a little flour; pour over the endive and let boil a few minutes to thicken slightly. Serve hot.

213
Dutch Meat and Egg Salad

2 large boiled potatoes, diced	1 small onion
1 cup of celery, diced	2 cloves of garlic finely
½ cup each of smoked hal-	minced
ibut, dried beef, and red	1 or 2 red peppers out of
smoked tongue all cut	pickle jar
small	6 hard boiled eggs

The dried beef and tongue should be cooked first by boiling several hours. The celery is better if blanched. Mix all, except the eggs, in a bowl and shake about with oil poured in till the mixture looks rich and glossy. Then add a cup of vinegar. Ornament with the yolks of eggs chopped fine and the whites cut in strips.

214
Dutch Herring Salad

1 or 2 large smoked herrings	1 cup of slices salsify or
1 cup of pickled red cabbage,	oyster plant
chopped small	1 cup of chopped white
pepper, salt, oil, vinegar	cabbage

Free the meat of the herrings from bones and skin and mince it as nearly in dice shapes as may be. The salsify may be substituted with potatoes; if necessary, cut in dice or lozenge shape. Mix all with oil, vinegar, pepper, and salt.

215
Dutch Jerusalem Salad

3 lbs. Jerusalem artichokes	½ cup green pepper, chopped
2 cups chopped celery	Lettuce, mayonnaise

Wash and boil in salted water the artichokes in their skins until tender. Dice them and combine with the celery and pepper. Serve cold with mayonnaise on lettuce.

216
Herring and Apple Salad

4 tart apples	1 onion
3 tablespoons vinegar	4 tablespoons walnuts
3 milch herrings	1 teaspoon sugar

Core and peel the apples, chop fine and mix with 2 tablespoons of the vinegar. Mince the onion and add, together with walnuts, minced, and the sugar. Remove skin and bones of herring after having soaked in several waters for 2 hours. Chop the herring into half-inch pieces. Mash the milch of the herring with one tablespoon of vinegar. Put through a strainer, and add to the herring pieces and the apples. Mix well. Taste and see that it is sour-sweet—adding more sugar or vinegar if necessary. Serve with lettuce and sliced hard boiled eggs.

217
Endive Salad, Black Horse Inn

6 or 8 potatoes	1 small stalk celery
2 or 3 stalks bleached endive	sour cream sauce

Parboil the potatoes and dice when cold, and add the endive and celery, diced. Pour over this a dressing made of 1 cup (or more) vinegar, salt, sugar and pepper, 1 tablespoon butter, one egg, beaten, ¼ cup sour cream. Boil and stir until it thickens. Then add the potatoes, endive and celery and heat thoroughly, but stir and don't let boil.

218
Hot Slaw, Pastorius

3 eggs	1½ tablespoons sugar
3 cups shredded cabbage	½ cup vinegar
1 tablespoon butter	½ cup cream (or milk)
1 teaspoon salt	⅛ teaspoon paprika

After shredding the cabbage blanche it in boiling water for 10 minutes. Drain and pour cold water over it in colander. Then cook in boiling water until tender. Make a mixture of the butter, vinegar, eggs, salt, sugar, cream, and paprika in half a cup of boiling water, and cook this in a double boiler, stirring, until thick. Add the cabbage and heat.

219
Dutch Horseradish Sauce

1 egg	1 tablespoon butter
½ cup horseradish	½ teaspoon salt
¼ cup cream (or milk)	¼ teaspoon paprika
1 teaspoon flour	

Freshly grate the horseradish root and cook until smooth in a glass or earthen vessel together with the flour, salt, butter and paprika. Keep stirring the mixture. Add the yolk of the egg and keep stirring rapidly while placing it to the rear of the stove to simmer for one half minute. Serve with meats, etc. as elsewhere indicated.

220
Dutch Oyster Salad

1 quart fresh oysters	1 pint chopped lettuce
1 pint chopped celery	Dutch Salad Cream

Drain off the liquor from the oysters; half or quarter them. Mix with the celery and lettuce. Pour over this the Dutch Salad Cream, recipe for which is included in this book.

Pennsylvania Dutch Pies

Whoever is doomed to eat only our modern "railroad station restaurant pie" or factory pie is doomed indeed! Good pie is almost an American invention, and the Dutch had a big finger in that pie invention! Of all the delights of Dutch cookery, I like best to think of one of my grandmother's slip-decorated earthen pie plates (*poi schuessel,* now collected as antiques), containing a green tomato pie, or blackberry, and pushed into the Dutch oven and coming out "sizzling" hot and redolent. What a pie!

The Dutch brought the art of pie-making to a very fine point through these earthen pie plates and Dutch oven technique. They made pies large and deep—I think it is likely that they were the very first to do so. They made pies with unique filler materials, and they dared even to make pies out of dried apples and peaches. This is surely a test for any cook, for nobody thinks of dried apples as interesting pie material.

In the *Saturday Evening Post* April, 1935, Edwin Leferre brings out the fact that the Dutch were the creators in America of the fruit pies so popular today and deserve credit for making pie the great American dish that it is.

The Dutch cooks used lard—but beautifully pure and well rendered home made lard. Also in the olden days they had flour which was milled by real millstones, not the superfine dust-like product of today's flour machinery. They used their hands deftly to make the crust.

Their green currant pies, green tomato pies, blackberry pies, pumpkin pies, rhubarb pies, gooseberry pies, plum pies, sour cherry pies, grape pies, strawberry pies, elderberry pies are delights, and some of them novelties to pie bakers. They have other novelties, too; the schnitz pie, the rhubarb custard pie, the country molasses pie, the mock cherry pie, the apple custard pie, the lemon pie, the *schleck* pie, the potato custard pie, the butterscotch pie, the crumb pie, etc.

They have also some oddities such as *fried pies*—not nearly so terrible as it sounds! It is fried in deep fat. Also Onion Cake.

In pot-pies they also revel, I like their Apple Pot Pie and their Squab Pot Pie.

As to mince pies, I verily believe they have a special gift. Theirs is not a mock-mince. One of the best varieties is compounded of calves' tongues, raisins, currants, citron, orange and lemon peel, even grated almonds. They put brandy or whisky into it. Then there is another variety, a Green Tomato Mince Meat. Another old recipe has beef in it, and boiled-down cider.

What the Dutch do to Pumpkin Pie is also rather remarkable, as is to be seen in the recipe.

Altogether, I believe Dutch cookery shines especially in pie bakery. Alas, that the earthen *poi schuessel* and the Dutch oven cannot be at the service of my readers, to reproduce their art more perfectly!

221
Molasses Pie, Neversink

1 cup molasses	1 cup bread crumbs, fine
6 tablespoons brown sugar	1 cup seedless raisins
½ lemon (rind only)	6 tablespoons flour
3 tablespoons flour	4 tablespoons brown sugar
1 teaspoon cinnamon	2 tablespoons shortening

Line a pie pan with pie crust. Spread over it the bread crumbs, and over these the raisins. Then place all the rest of the ingredients listed in the first column above, and mix. Pour this mixture over the pie. Then mix, in a second bowl, the ingredients listed in the *second* column above. Make into fine crumbs with the fingers. Spread over the pie. Then make inch-wide strips of pie-crust and spread them criss-cross over the pie. Bake in a slow oven.

222
Dutch Black Walnut Pie

4 eggs	1¼ cups Karo syrup
3 tablespoons flour	1 cup black walnuts
1½ cups sugar	

Make a pie crust for two pies and line medium sized pie plates with it. Sprinkle the walnuts over the crusts, and then dip into them the filling made of the above ingredients well mixed. The eggs must be well-beaten before adding the sugar gradually, then fold in flour, followed by Karo and 1½ cups of water, and well stirred. Bake in a very hot oven for 3 minutes and then reduce to medium for 30 or 40 minutes.

223
Cream Raspberry Pie

After lining a pie plate with pie-crust, fill it with red raspberries. Cover with granulated sugar and with an upper crust, but rub the edges of both upper and lower crust with butter so they won't stick together. Then when the pie is baked, let it get cold, and make ready a cream with 1 cup of milk and 1 teaspoon of cornstarch and 2 tablespoons sugar. Cook this and when cool add the whites of 3 eggs stiffly beaten. Lift up the upper crust of the pie and pour in this cream. Replace the upper crust, and sift over it powdered sugar.

224
Molasses Pie, Schnockaschtettle

1 cup flour	¼ cup molasses
½ cup sugar	¼ teaspoon baking soda
1½ tablespoons butter	pie crust

Mix well flour, sugar and butter, to make "crumbs." Mix the molasses together with ¼ cup boiling water and the baking soda. Beat until foamy. Pour into a pie plate lined with pie crust, and sprinkle the crumbs into the mixture. Bake 30 minutes in medium hot oven.

225
Green Currant Pie, Plum Creek

After lining a pie dish with pie crust sprinkle the bottom with 2½ tablespoons of sugar and 2 tablespoons flour (or 1 of cornstarch), mixed. Then pour in 1 pint of washed green currants and 2 tablespoons currant jelly. Sprinkle this with 7 tablespoons of sugar, and pour over it 2 tablespoons of water. Cover with upper crust and bake.

226
Green Currant Pie, Cocallico

2 cups green currants	1 tablespoon cornstarch
1 cup sugar	2 tablespoons of flour

Wash the currants in two cold waters, add the cornstarch mixed with a little cold water. Then add nearly all the cup of sugar, and two tablespoons of water. Have ready a rich pie crust, placing the flour and two tablespoons from the cup of sugar on the bottom crust. Cover with another crust, bake in medium hot oven.

227
Dutch Green Tomato Mince Meat

1 peck green tomatoes	1 teaspoon cloves
5 lbs. sugar	1½ tablespoons grated
3 lemons	nutmeg
2 pounds seedless raisins	1 tablespoon cinnamon
½ cup grated orange peel,	1 cup vinegar
citron	1 cup cider

Chop the tomatoes and cook nearly 4 hours, after which add all the other ingredients and cook for 30 minutes. Place hot in glass jars for use as desired. Bake like mince pies.

228
Parsley Pie (Mouldasha)

6 potatoes	1 cup flour
1 onion	1 cup milk
1 teaspoon minced parsley	1 egg
1 teaspoon baking powder	2 teaspoons salt
2 teaspoons butter	

Mix flour, baking powder and salt. Mix separately with potatoes mashed and mixed with butter, onion (grated) and the parsley. Mix milk and egg, with the flour and make a soft dough. Roll out thin, cut into 8 inch squares, and place on them the potato mixture, turning over the dough and closing the edges. Put the filled squares in boiling water until they rise to surface. Lift out and brown them in buttered pans. Serve hot.

229
Dutch Crumb Pie (Rivel Kuche)

1 cup flour	½ teaspoon grated nutmeg
1 scant cup sugar	2 tablespoons molasses
½ cup butter	

Mix sugar, flour and butter together with the nutmeg, converting the mixture with the hands into a collection of lumps (rivels). Make a good pie crust, line pie plates with it and spread the rivels over them. Pour the molasses over the rivels. Bake in hot oven.

230
Dutch Grape Pie

5 lbs. grapes	2 tablespoons flour
1 cup sugar	Pie crust
1 teaspoon butter	

Remove skins and mash the grapes and cook for 15 minutes. Remove seeds, odd skins, and the sugar and butter. Line pie plates with crust, sprinkle with tablespoon of flour. Place in mixture, sprinkle with another tablespoon of flour. Cover with crust.

231
Dutch Sour Cherry Pie

1 quart fresh sour cherries	½ cup flour
1½ cups sugar	

Remove cherry stones, saving juice. Mix flour and sugar; placing a third of this mixture on bottom of pie tin, after it has been lined with rich crust. Then fill with the cherries and sprinkle on top the other two-thirds of the mixture. Put on a top pie crust, vented, and bake in medium hot oven.

232
Dutch Strawberry Pie

3 quarts strawberries	1 cup sugar
½ cup flour	1 teaspoon butter

Wash strawberries in cold water, hull and mix sugar with them. Place in three pie tins, lined with rich pie crust, sprinkling flour over the berries and at edges. Place dots of butter over the berries and cover with top crust, vented.

233
Dutch Apple-Lemon Custard Pie

1 apple	2 eggs
1 lemon	pie crust
1½ cups sugar	

Pare and grate the apple, and grate also the rind of half a lemon, also the rest of the lemon. Add the sugar and 2 beaten eggs. Bake covered pie style with pie crust in medium hot oven. Sift with powdered sugar.

234
Dutch Rhubarb Custard

5 stalks rhubarb	2 eggs
1 cup sugar	Pie crust
1 tablespoon cornstarch	1 tablespoon powdered sugar

Cut rhubarb in small dices. Mix the sugar, cornstarch and eggs (keeping in reserve the white of one egg). Add the rhubarb and bake custard-style on pastry crust, in medium hot oven. When finished and pie is cool, place on top the stiffly beaten white of one egg, plus one tablespoon of powdered sugar. Put back in oven for browning.

235
Dutch Potato Custard

1 large potato	2 tablespoons butter
1 scant cup sugar	2 eggs
1 cup milk	½ lemon
pie curst	

Boil and mash the potato, add the butter and sugar, and mix to creamy consistency. Set to cool, add yolks of eggs and milk.

Grate the rind of half a lemon, add its juice, and place in mixture, then fold in the whites of eggs, beaten stiff. Bake custard style on one pastry crust in medium hot oven for 30 minutes, until brown.

236
Peach Custard Pie, Pottstown

Fresh peaches	½ teaspoon cornstarch
2 eggs, beaten	1 pint whole milk
¾ cup sugar	Grated nutmeg

Line a pie plate with pie crust, and lay on it one layer of the peaches, peeled and sliced. Then add to the beaten eggs the sugar and cornstarch, and stir well. Then add the milk. Pour this over the peaches; sprinkle with nutmeg. Bake in hot oven.

237'
Dutch Union Pie
(*Makes* 4 *Pies*)

1 cup molasses	1 cup thick milk
1 cup sour cream	2 eggs, beaten
1 cup brown sugar	3 tablespoons flour
1 teaspoon salt	1 teaspoon baking soda

Make a mixture of these ingredients, and add the spices. Line a pie plate with pie crust, pour in the mixture, and lay strips criss-cross over the pie.

238
Pumpkin Pie, Delaware Water Gap
(*Makes* 3 *Pies*)

3 eggs, beaten	1 teaspoon cinnamon
1 cup sugar	¼ teaspoon ginger
3 cups pumpkin	¼ teaspoon nutmeg
(or Hubbard Squash)	2 tablespoons brandy
½ teaspoon salt	2 cups milk

Stew the pumpkin or squash tender, drain well and mash through colander. Mix with the beaten eggs the sugar, salt and spices and the milk and brandy. Mix with pumpkin. Pour into pie plates lined with pie crust, and bake in moderate oven.

239
Lemon Sponge Pie

2 egg yolks,　　　　　　　2 heaping tablespoons flour
1 cup sugar　　　　　　　Little salt
Juice and rind of 1 lemon

Beat egg yolks thoroughly, add one cup milk and the beaten whites of the eggs, and bake in pastry shell for about 40 minutes.

240
Cheese Pie

Use cottage cheese mashed very fine, or two packages of Philadelphia cream cheese. Add 2 tablespoons of thick cream, 2 tablespoons butter, ¼ teaspoon salt, ¾ cup sugar, 2 tablespoons flour, 1 cup milk, one well beaten egg and the juice and grated rind of ½ lemon. Beat well. Bake on pie crust in moderate oven.

241
Snitz Pie (Dried Apple Pie)

Snitz have to be soaked over night and then boiled. You have to keep adding water so that by the time the snitz are tender and can be stirred up it is the consistency of real thick apple sauce. When boiling the snitz, cut in a little orange peel (rind), about a half a teaspoon to a pie. When apples are soft, season with cinnamon and sugar to taste and bake in a pie with a top crust, or with criss-cross strips of dough across the top. You don't want too many snitz in the pie—about one half inch deep.

242
Pumpkin Pie

1 cup cooked, pressed, pumpkin	2 cups milk
½ cup sugar	¼ teaspoon salt
2 tablespoons molasses	½ teaspoon ginger
3 eggs	1 teaspoon cinnamon

Bake in pie, uncovered, or with criss-cross strips of crust across the top.

243
Dutch Corn Pie

Line a casserole with pastry (not quite as rich as for a pie). Into this put a can of corn (not crushed) mixed with four or five chopped hard boiled eggs and seasoned with salt and pepper. Scatter a good tablespoon of flour over the top. Put dabs of butter around and enough milk to almost cover the corn and then cover with an upper crust.

Bake in a hot oven for about an hour.

244
Dutch Huckleberry Pie

After lining a pie plate with pie crust, put in a quart of huckleberries, which have been washed well and picked for stems and green berries. There should be a half inch depth of berries. Pour ½ cup sugar over the berries, 1 teaspoon of flour, ½ teaspoon salt, and then grate some nutmeg over it. Slit the pie. Bake 30 minutes in hot oven.

245
Dutch Plum Pie

2 or 3 cups green gage plums (or other plums), pie crust	1 teaspoon cinnamon
1 or ½ cup sugar	2 tablespoons corn meal or cornflakes, powdered sugar

Prepare the pie crust and line the pie pan with it. Sprinkle the cornmeal or cornflakes on it. Halve or quarter the plums, lay them on the crust, and sprinkle the sugar and cinnamon over them. Bake in moderate oven and when done, sprinkle with powdered sugar.

246
Dutch Shoofly Pie

1 cup molasses	½ teaspoon salt
4 cups flour	2 cups sugar
½ cup butter and lard	1 teaspoon baking soda
	½ teaspoon cream of tartar

Dissolve the molasses in 1 cup of water. Mix all other ingredients and form into crumbs. Pour molasses mixture into pans lined with pie crust, then spread the crumbs evenly on top. Sprinkle with cinnamon and bake in moderate oven.

247
Shrew-Berry, Susquehanna

4½ cups flour	1 teaspoon cinnamon
1 lb. sugar	½ teaspoon ginger
¼ lb. butter	1 teaspoon baking soda
2 eggs	½ teaspoon ground cloves

Mix the ingredients, except the eggs, which then add, well beaten. Roll out and cut into cookie form.

248
Chicken Cornmeal Pie, Oley

1 cup cornmeal	1 chicken
2 eggs	1 teaspoon salt
½ cup milk	½ teaspoon pepper
	4 strips bacon

Sift the cornmeal twice. Beat the eggs well, mix with the milk, and add the cornmeal, and form a batter. Line a pie pan with pie dough, and put half the cornmeal mixture into it. Sprinkle over it the pepper and salt. Have ready a parboiled chicken, sliced into flat pieces. Put these in the pie pan, place on top of them the strips of bacon. Place on top of it the remainder of the cornmeal mixture and bake in a hot oven.

249
Squab Pot Pie, Cacoosing

2 squabs	1 onion, chopped
4 potatoes, diced	1 tablespoon chopped parsley

Use an iron pot, if you have one, or steam cooker. Split the squabs. Then in the pot place first a layer of potatoes, then a layer of chopped onion and parsley, then a layer of squab, rubbed with pepper and salt, and on top of the mixture put some pie crust dough (made with two teaspoons of baking powder added to each cup of flour), this dough cut into four-inch squares. If larger quantity of pot pie is wanted, repeat another series of layers. Then add a pint of water (more if iron pot is used) and boil gently for 2 hours. Serve hot.

250
Potato Sausage Pie, Cacoosing

6 or 8 potatoes	1 lb. Mickelberry sausage
1 onion	filling
	1 teaspoon minced parsley

Dice the potatoes, peel the onions. Put into boiling salted water and boil for 8 minutes. Then drain except for two cupfuls of water. Place in deep casserole or glass baking dish, making layers of potato and sausage. Sprinkle with parsley. When two-thirds filled add the water (it should rise to one half the height of the material). Put rich pie crust over the top and bake in hot oven.

251
Dutch Cabbage Pork Pie

¾ lb. chopped pork	2 tablespoons butter
¾ lb. chopped beef	½ teaspoon pepper
1 head cabbage	1 teaspoon salt
2 eggs	

Take off the rough outside leaves of the cabbage, also the core. Boil until tender in salted water. Make a mixture of the beef, pork, butter, eggs and seasoning. Drain the water from the cabbage, butter a pudding mold, put in the dish alternate layers of cabbage leaves and meat, ending with cabbage on top. Close the mold, put in a steamer over boiling water and boil for 2 hours. Drain off broth and lay on platter. Make a gravy with a tablespoon of butter, 5 crackers crumbed or some flour, salt, pepper and broth. Boil it; if too thick add more broth. Stir in two yolks of eggs. Serve hot with the pie.

252
Goose Liver Pie

3 large goose livers	2 tablespoons of Madeira or
¾ lb. fat pork	red wine
¾ lb. veal	salt
6 truffles	pepper
1½ lemon	3 yolks of eggs
⅛ lb. of butter	1 teaspoon grated onion
⅔ pt. of bouillon	bacon slices to line the pan
	4 tablespoons of flour

Take two of the goose livers and lard with oblong slices of peeled truffles. Drip the juice from 1½ lemons on the livers and let stand for several hours.

Heat the butter and mix with the flour, salt and pepper and ¾ pt. of broth. Add the Madeira. Stir into the thick gravy the finely chopped or ground veal and pork. Chop one goose liver and fry 2 minutes in 2 tablespoonfuls of butter and the onion. Add salt and pepper and mix into the filling. Fill all this into a deep baking pan or mold lined with bacon slices so that it makes 2 to 3 layers of stuffing, alternating with slices of goose liver. Cover with slices of bacon, set in steamer over a kettle of boiling water and boil for 1½ hours or bake in oven for 1 hour. Serve with Madeira or truffle gravy.

253
Dutch Chicken Corn Pie

Cut a spring chicken and stew it for 15 minutes. Make a good puff paste and line the sides of a deep baking dish with it; then put in the bottom a layer of chicken and cover well with green corn, cut from the cob; or Shaker dried corn, soaked for 12 hours in water. Season with pepper, salt, and plenty of butter.

Fill the dish in this manner and add the water in which the chicken was boiled; cover the top with the pastry, vented, and bake in a moderate oven.

11

Dutch Dumplings, Fritters, Pancakes, Etc.

In these the Dutch have always revelled. They relied on flour in cookery quite as frequently as did Southern cooks with their hot biscuits, pot-pies and pancakes.

The dumpling was easily the favorite, and the famous *schnitz und Knepp* relied as heavily upon the dumplings as upon the apples. I know of no other cuisine in which dumplings are so freely used and in such a variety of combinations. The liver dumplings are a special delicacy.

Lard was very widely used by the Dutch because they rendered it themselves. They made it as pure and harmless as they knew how; but of course nowadays most people prefer lard substitutes of vegetable oil origin.

They made dumplings of liver, dumplings of potatoes, dumplings of rice, dumplings of corn, dumplings of prunes, etc. And as for fritters, their parsnip fritter alone is a grand original contribution to the art of cookery; while their elderberry kuklein is worthy of the most esoteric French member of the Cordon Bleu. Even the ordinary fritters (apple, banana, green corn, etc.) are given a special twist that rather differentiates them. For additional oddities, what could be more unique than their *Boova Shenkel* or their *Mouldasha?* And their taste is widely attested to in Pennsylvania.

The Dutch are fond of all forms of pancakes. I do not believe I have ever met their equal in buckwheat cakes or egg-pancakes or buttermilk waffles or plain *pfannkuchen.* Flannel cakes from sour milk are also very good.

Waffles and Pancakes, Custards, etc.

Such oddities as Lemon Toast, Schnecken haus'ln, Funnel Cakes, Moravian Sugar Cakes, Snow Balls, Flash Un Kas, Cheese Custard, Strickle Sheets, Streusel Kuchen, Fried Pies, etc., are all well worth eating and unique cooking accomplishments.

254
Dutch Egg Pfannkuchen

4 eggs	2 tablespoons butter
2 tablespoons milk	$\frac{1}{2}$ teaspoon salt
1 teaspoon chopped parsley	

Beat whites and yolks separately, add milk and parsley, mix, add salt. Melt butter in clean frying pan, pour in the batter, and when cooked, sprinkle with parsley. Serve rolled and hot.

255
Corn Pancakes (Welshkorn Pfannkuchen)

1 cup milk	1 tablespoon butter
4 tablespoons cornmeal	2 tablespoons flour
$\frac{1}{2}$ teaspoon salt	2 teaspoons baking powder

Scald milk, stir in cornmeal, add butter When cool stir in flour, adding enough cold milk to make batter, add baking powder. Fry on hot greased griddle.

256
Corn Meal Mush and Kidneys, Kuechler's Roost

The corn meal mush itself must be made in a particular way. You moisten two cups of corn meal and two tablespoons of flour with cold water enough to make a paste. Then have ready a pot of furiously boiling salted water. Put in the cornmeal paste, stirring constantly, then cook in a double boiler for 3 to 4 hours. When done pour into oblong bread pans. When cold, it is ready to cut into slices.

You do *not* fry it—you *bake* it in buttered pans. The slices must first however be brushed with milk or cream, and rolled in bread crumbs. Bake brown.

Meanwhile you take lamb kidneys which have been skinned and split, and the center tube taken out (but not the little piece of fat). You drop them into boiling water for a few minutes to sear the outside and keep the gravy in, and then fry them in bacon fat, constantly turning them. The fire should not be very hot. Then pour a bit of water in the pan and a teaspoon or so of flour and make a gravy. Serve the kidneys on top of the corn meal mush slices, sprinkled with chopped parsley, and the gravy poured on.

257
Flannel Cakes and Sausage, Steigerwald

2 eggs	1 tablespoon butter
1½ cups sour cream or buttermilk	1 teaspoon baking soda
1½ cups sweet milk	1½ lbs. Dutch smoked beef sausages (or any other
3 cups flour	sausages)

Make a batter of the above ingredients, putting the soda in the sour milk or buttermilk, and beating the eggs separately. Bake on hot griddle. Meanwhile fry the sausages in pieces, and when finished make a gravy with milk and little flour. Serve piping hot with sausage and gravy over the flannel cake.

258
Buckwheat Cakes and Blackstrap, Christopher Ludwig

⅔ cake yeast
1½ cups buckwheat flour
½ cup white flour

1 teaspoon salt
½ teaspoon sugar
Blackstrap molasses (or any molasses or syrup)

Break up the ⅔ cake of yeast, and put in one half cup of luke-warm water, with ½ teaspoon sugar. Let this bubble, then mix it well with the two flours, the salt and enough cold water to a delicate but stiff batter, beaten. Let this rise for 3 to 4 hours, covered with a cloth, in warm spot. (If to be used for breakfast, let dough rise overnight, but then you do not wait for yeast cake to bubble—it is merely dissolved and at once put into dough).

Then there should be added 1½ tablespoons of blackstrap (or other molasses), and the griddle prepared—cleaned and heated, rubbed with salt, and then greased with a piece of *fresh* pork or butter. Let griddle get smoking hot. Have spoon ready of a size to hold just enough batter to make cakes about 4 inches in dia-meter, no more. Serve piping hot with blackstrap or other mo-lasses or syrup. (Blackstrap or dark molasses is still sold, and it is a better molasses than any other.)

259
Buckwheat Cakes and Smoked Sausages, Half-way House

2 cups good buckwheat flour
1 tablespoon salt
1 yeast cake

2 tablespoons brown sugar
2 cups buttermilk

After dissolving the yeast in a little lukewarm water, mix the ingredients together to form a batter and let rise overnight, for use at the next morning's breakfast— (also the following morn-ing's breakfast, and so for two weeks; each night adding a cup-ful of flour, plus buttermilk enough to make batter and letting rise each night; each third day adding ½ teaspoon of salt and a teaspoon of sugar).

Fry smoked Dutch beef sausages and make a gravy with the

fat, thickening with flour. The smoked beef sausages are sold anywhere in Dutch farm markets and meat shops; or use any sausages, pork or beef, fresh or smoked.

260
Pfannkuchen, Bernville

6 cups flour	1 cake yeast
½ cup butter, melted	4 tablespoons sugar
1 cup warm milk	1 teaspoon salt
3 eggs, well beaten	½ cup currant jelly

Dissolve in a bowl the yeast in a little of the warm milk, with a little flour mixed in. When this bubbles, add it to the flour, milk, eggs, sugar, salt and butter. Beat until it forms blisters, and make into a thick sponge. Cover the bowl with cloth and set in a warm place to rise to double its size. Then flour a bread board and roll out to one half inch thickness. Cut out with round cookie cutter. Place a half teaspoon of the jelly in the center of half of them and then lay the others on top, pressing the sides. Have ready hot deep fat, in a deep frying pan. Fry until brown and double their size. Drain on absorbent paper and serve hot —yes, even for breakfast, in the good old Dutch tradition. It is after all only a bread, and not as heavy as the hot biscuits of Southern cookery, if carefully made. It makes good "dunking" in coffee.

261
Dutch Buckwheat Cakes

2 tablespoons corn meal	1 tablespoon molasses
2 tablespoons buckwheat flour (best quality, fresh)	1½ qts. potato water
1 pint warm water	2 tablespoons mashed potatoes
1 teaspoon baking soda	2 teaspoons salt
	1 cup warm milk

Dissolve yeast in warm water, add corn meal and buckwheat flour, to consistency of batter. Let rise in warm place for 6 or 7 hours. Then add to it potato water, mashed potatoes, salt. Then bring to batter consistency with more buckwheat flour, beat well, and set to rise over night. In morning, add baking soda (dissolved in warm water), molasses and enough warm milk to thin batter. After standing half hour fry on extra hot griddle.

262
Dutch Parsnip Fritters

6 young parsnips	2 tablespoons flour
1 egg	¼ teaspoon baking powder
½ teaspoon salt	

Scrape off skin of parsnips, boil in salted water. Mash, add egg yolk, and then the separately beaten white. Then add flour, baking powder and salt, roll into cakes, dredge with flour or cornmeal, and fry in butter. Serve sizzling hot. Alternative way is to grate the parsnips, add egg yolk and salt, tablespoon of milk, then fold in the well beaten white of egg.

263
Elderberry Blossom Cakes (*Heller Bluther Kuchlein*)

1 bunch elderberry blossoms	1 bowl of standard fritter batter

Rinse the blossoms, let dry, then while holding the stems, dip the blossoms into standard fritter batter, after which drop them into smoking hot fat until batter is golden brown. Drain upon absorbent paper napkins, dust with powdered sugar and cinnamon.

264
Dutch Apple Fritters (*Apel Kuche*)

5 tart apples	1 cup flour
3 tablespoons cider	½ teaspoon baking powder
½ teaspoon cinnamon	2 eggs
1 teaspoon sugar	1 cup milk

Core and pare the apples, and then cut into circular slices ½ inch thick. Soak them for two hours in a mixture of cider, cinnamon, sugar. Drain and dry with clean towel. Make batter of flour, baking powder, adding the yolks of the eggs and milk, then mixing in the beaten whites. Dip the apples in the batter and fry in butter. Dust with sugar before serving.

265
Dutch Potato Cakes (*Grumbera Kuche*)

2 eggs
1 small onion
1 teaspoon minced parsley

3 potatoes
1 slice whole wheat bread

Pare and boil the potatoes and mash them (or use left-over mashed potatoes). Mix well with them the onion, minced, the bread, crumbed, the eggs and the parsley. Mould into paste and fry to golden brown on a hot griddle, greased with butter, or butter and Crisco mixed.

266
Dutch Funnel Cakes

Mix 1 pint of sweet milk, 2 eggs well beaten, (yolks and whites together), enough flour to make a thin batter, ½ teaspoonful baking powder, ¼ teaspoonful salt. Mix in a pan thoroughly. Place enough lard in a pan to cover the bottom. Let it get quite hot before cooking the batter. Now put the batter through a funnel into the hot lard, beginning at center of pan, and turning the stream around in a gradually enlarging circle, being careful not to touch the sides or the other dough. Fry a light brown and serve hot with any tart jelly.

267
Lancaster Cornmeal Mush

Mix 3 cups cornmeal with 3 cups cold water. Heat, then add 12 cups of boiling water, stirring all the time that it may not become lumpy; add salt to taste.

Boil for 35 minutes over a steady fire. When done pour into molds. Slice when cold into thin slices; fry in butter or vegetable shortening in a pan or griddle, together with strips of bacon.

268
Dutch Onion Fritters

2 Bermuda onions   Fritter batter, cinnamon

Slice the onion into rings of about ¼ inch width, and separate into individual rings. Soak these for 1½ hours in cold water. Drain and dry. Dip into the batter and fry in deep fat. Sprinkle lightly with cinnamon and serve hot.

269
Breakfast, Pennypacker
(*Buckwheat cakes, Tomatoes, Sausages*)

To make the buckwheat cakes, follow these special directions: Mix together 1 tablespoon flour, 1 tablespoon molasses, ½ teaspoon salt. Dissolve a yeast cake in lukewarm water, add it to the above mixture and stir smooth. Then mix in 1 pint of milk, and then 1 quart good buckwheat flour. Let stand overnight. In the morning add ¼ teaspoon baking soda. Thin the mixture if too stiff. Pour batter on hot greased griddle.

Grill tomatoes, or fry them rolled in flour or cracker dust, and serve with fresh beef or pork sausages.

270
Dutch Cheese Noodles

1 cup cottage cheese	1 cup sour milk
3 eggs	1 teaspoon baking soda
⅛ lb. butter	Flour

Make a soft dough of the ingredients and roll out flat, about 1 inch thick. Cut into pieces four inches by one inch. Fry in deep fat. Sprinkle with sugar and cinnamon.

271
Dutch Corn Waffles

¼ cup Shaker dried corn (or
    ¾ cup green corn off the
    cob, or good canned
    corn)
2 eggs
1 cup milk

1 tablespoon melted butter
1½ cups ·flour
2 teaspoons baking powder
1 teaspoon sugar
½ teaspoon salt

Beat the egg-whites stiff; beat the egg yolks thin. Then add the
milk, butter and corn (grated or pulped) to the egg yolks, after
which stir this into the flour, baking powder, sugar and salt after
sifting together. Fold in the egg-whites, and bake in hot waffle
iron (only half filling the lower mold). Serve hot with crisp bacon and syrup. (The Shaker corn must be soaked in lukewarm
water for about 12 hours in advance and pulped.)

272
Dutch Jerusalem Fritters

10 Jerusalem artichokes
    1 egg

1 cup flour

Boil and mash the artichokes, let cool, and then add the yolk
of the egg. Mold into cakes, dip in the flour and fry in butter on
a hot griddle.

273
Kartoffle Glace, Bucks

4 potatoes
2 eggs
Flour

1 teaspoon salt
1 tablespoon butter
½ cup fine bread crumbs

Boil the potatoes in their skins, cool, peel and put through the
meat grinder. Add the salt and the eggs and flour enough to
make a stiff batter. Roll out into balls about an inch or less in
diameter. Cook in water, and then place in a frying pan with
the butter after melting and heat with the bread crumbs. Serve
hot, with boiled beef, potroast, or almost anything.

12

The Dutch
"Seven Sweets and Seven Sours"

There never was a more indefatigable preserver, pickler, curer, spicer, or canner than the Dutch housewife. Very little escapes her expert touch—and as a consequence she got in the habit centuries ago of loading every table with many "sweets and sours."

To such an extent that over the centuries it became a fixed tradition of Dutch hospitality for her to put on the table (especially for "company") *precisely seven sweets and seven sours.* The "company" would often count them! indeed would gaily demand them if missing.

I have always maintained that a variety of sweets and sours on the table was a distinct gastronomic delight and digestive aid. Most of the Germanic peoples of the south of Germany, in particular the Hungarians, have always been fond of sweets and sours on the table. The Swedes, and perhaps also the Italians and French, like them at the beginning of the meal; but my own appetite reaction is for having them during the meal, to relieve the cloying taste of quantities of protein and starch. But perhaps I was early conditioned to the Dutch way.

The Dutch variety of sweets and sours is the most extensive I have ever contacted with. The range of course includes all the standard things known to other cuisines, and I have therefore included only those which offer some little special Dutch touch in the making.

274
Spiced Peaches

3 lbs. peaches, 1½ lbs. sugar, ½ cup vinegar, 5 or 6 sticks cinnamon bark. Dissolve vinegar and sugar, then throw in the peaches, when soft enough to pierce with a straw, take out and add 1 doz. cloves, and cinnamon bark to the syrup. Boil well and pour over the peaches.

275
Dutch Spiced Red Cabbage

2 heads red cabbage	1 teaspoon celery seed
½ cup salt	1 teaspoon pepper
1 gallon vinegar	1 teaspoon each mace, **all-**
1 cup sugar	spice, cinnamon

Shred the cabbage, sprinkle with the salt, let stand 24 hours. Press moisture out, stand in sun for 3 hours. Boil for 8 minutes the vinegar, with ½ cup water, the sugar and the spices, and while hot pour over the cabbage. Keep in large bowl or earthen jar.

276
Dutch Spiced Cucumbers

20 cucumbers	3 green peppers
4 red peppers	½ cup salt
5 onions	1 quart vinegar
1 teaspoon turmeric powder	1 tablespoon cloves
1 cup sugar	

After pealing the cucumbers, do not slice but cut the long way into inch long slabs. Thinly slice onions and peppers. Put these in large bowl, sprinkle the salt over them and mix. After letting stand four hours, drain through colander, and then squeeze juices out through cheese cloth. Then boil the vinegar, cloves, turmeric powder (first dissolved in a little vinegar) and the sugar. Then add the cucumbers to this liquid and boil for two or three minutes. Place in glass jars.

277
Dutch Ginger Pears

5 lbs. hard pears	4 lbs. brown sugar
2 lemons	$\frac{1}{4}$ lb. ginger root

Peel and core the pears, and cut into quarters. Cut the lemon rind into strings, and put them with the pears, including the lemon juice, in kettle. Cook slowly for an hour, until clear. Pack in glass jars.

278
Dutch Applebutter (Lotwaerick)

$\frac{1}{2}$ bushel apples	3 lbs. brown sugar
5 gallons cider	$1\frac{1}{2}$ oz. allspice

Boil down the cider, with sugar and allspice, to $2\frac{1}{2}$ gallons, then add the pared and cored apples. If the apples are tart, add more sugar. Stir the mess *constantly* until it is of moderately thick consistency. Pack in glass jars.

279
Lancaster Applebutter in Quantity

Pare and quarter 2 bushels of apples and 1 peck of quinces. Cook the latter soft in water and mash through a colander. Boil and skim $\frac{1}{2}$ barrel of cider in large iron kettle until no froth gathers. Remove part of this cider, leaving in the kettle just enough to cook the apples soft. When they are soft, add the mashed quinces. As the mixture cooks pour in the rest of the cider, a little at a time. When the butter is of the desired thickness, add sugar to taste. Sugar thins the butter, hence the cooking must be continued until the butter again becomes as thick as desired. Just before removing the kettle from the fire, add cinnamon and cloves to taste.

280
Dutch Quince Honey

4 quinces   1 teaspoon diced lemon rind
3 lbs. sugar

Grate the quinces, after peeling, but eliminate the core. Then bring to a boil a mixture of 3 pints of water, and the sugar. Add lemon rind. Pour in the quince mixture, and boil for 25 minutes. Pack in small glass containers.

281
Dutch Rhubarb Jam

3 lbs. rhubarb   2 oranges
2 lbs. sugar

Cut rhubarb, after skinning, into small pieces, add the sugar and ½ cup cold water. Grate the rind of the oranges, mix with orange juice. Cook the entire mixture, for about 30 minutes, with occasional stirring.

282
Dutch Rhubarb Marmalade

25 stalks rhubarb   3 cups sugar
1 doz. almonds, blanched   1 lemon

Cut rhubarb into small pieces after skinning, cook with 1 cup water until tender. Mash the rhubarb, add the sugar (about 3 cups rhubarb to 1 of sugar), also the blanched and stewed almonds.

Cook for 15 minutes after adding the juice and grated rind of lemon.

283

Dutch Ripe Tomato Pickle

Boil together for one hour the following:

12 tomatoes, 3 sweet peppers, 2 tablespoons whole mustard seed, 1 cup sugar, 1 oz. celery seed, 3 hot peppers, 6 onions, 4 tablespoons salt, 3 cups vinegar, spice to taste.

284

Dutch Green Tomato Pickle

1 peck green tomatoes, 12 large onions, 12 large peppers.

Wash, cut into quarters, sprinkle with salt, and let stand over night. Then drain and cover with vinegar. Then add the following spices:

2 oz. mustard seed, $\frac{1}{2}$ oz. turmeric, $\frac{1}{2}$ oz. celery seed, $\frac{1}{2}$ oz. cloves, $\frac{1}{2}$ oz. allspice, $\frac{1}{2}$ oz. whole ginger, 3 lbs. brown sugar.

Then cook about 2 hours, add $\frac{1}{4}$ lb. Colman's mustard and thicken a little with flour.

285

Sweet Watermelon Pickle

Cut the rind into small pieces and soak it for three or four hours, then weigh it and to 5 pounds of it allow 3 pounds of granulated sugar and 3 pints of vinegar. Put the sugar and vinegar into a saucepan and bring it to a boil; skim well and add a spice bag containing nutmeg, stick cinnamon, mace and whole cloves, and let it cook for 4 minutes and pour it boiling hot over the rind. Allow to stand all night and next morning drain the syrup from the rind, boil it up once more with the spice bag, and again pour it over the rind. Repeat this process twice, after which put the entire mass, rind and all, into a preserving kettle and let it boil for 3 minutes; add the juice of four lemons well strained and cook for three minutes more. Then seal, boiling hot, in hot, sterilized fruit jars.

286

Spiced Cantaloupe

6 lbs. of cantaloupe cut as nearly one size as possible, 4 qts. of water, 1 oz. of alum; bring to the boiling point, drop in your fruit, cook 15 minutes, lift and drain a short while. Then take 1 qt. of vinegar, 3 lbs. of white sugar, 3 teaspoonfuls of yellow mustard seed, 1 teaspoonful of black mustard seed, 1 teaspoonful whole mace, 8 inch stick cinnamon, 9 whole cloves, about a doz. whole allspice. Place the fruit in it and slowly cook until clear; requires about 2 hours.

287

Green Tomato Soy

2 gals. green tomatoes, chopped without peeling, 12 good sized onions sliced, 2 qts. vinegar, 1 qt. sugar, 2 tablespoonfuls salt, 2 tablespoonfuls ground mustard, 2 tablespoonfuls black pepper, 1 tablespoonful allspice, 1 tablespoonful cloves.

Mix all together and stew until tender, stirring often lest they should scorch. Put in small glass jars.

288

Cucumber Chow-Chow

1 doz. large cucumbers, 4 large onions, and 1 small sharp pepper, cut fine, and lightly salted over night. In the morning squeeze out, add 1 small bunch of celery cut fine, some celery seed, and yellow mustard seed. Cover with vinegar and heat all together, but do not let come to a boil. Seal hot in glass jars.

289

Corn Chow-Chow

1 quart of vinegar, 1 quart of string beans, ½ doz. red peppers, 1 pint of lima beans, 1 pint of small onions, 1 doz. ears of corn, 2 tablespoonfuls of salt, ½ lb. of sugar, ¼ lb. of mustard. Mix

mustard and vinegar and bring to a scald. Cook separately the corn, onions, and beans till tender. Put all the ingredients together, boil only five minutes and seal.

290
Chow-Chow, Berks

6 large white onions, 6 large sweet peppers, red and green, 1 head of cabbage, ½ peck green tomatoes, 2 doz. medium sized cucumbers, 1 bunch celery, 1 head cauliflower, 1 pint small onions, and about 50 little pickles.

Slice the onions, cabbage and tomatoes on slaw cutter. Cut the peppers and cucumbers into small pieces. Put all of these with cauliflower into strong salt water and boil until tender, but not too soft. Then drain well through a sieve or colander. Put back into the kettle with the small onions, celery, and little pickles. The small pickles should stand in salt water several times before adding. Add to this ¼ pound of white mustard seed, tablespoonful of celery seed, handful each of cinnamon bark and whole allspice, some mace and pint of grated horse-radish, ½ gallon of cider vinegar.

Mix up some yellow mustard and add half a teaspoonful of turmeric, sweeten with brown sugar to taste. Mix all well and let come to a boil, then pack in jars, having the pickle well covered with the vinegar.

291
Chow-Chow, Montgomery

1 pk. green tomatoes, ½ pk. ripe tomatoes, 3 heads cabbage, ½ doz. green peppers, ½ doz. red peppers. Cut all and sprinkle with 1 cupful salt, let stand all night, next day strain and add 3 lbs. of sugar, 1 teacupful grated horse-radish, cover with vinegar and let come to a boil; then add 1 tablespoonful black pepper, 1 tablespoonful ground mustard and 1 tablespoonful of mustard seed, 1 tablespoonful ground cloves, 1 tablespoonful mace, and 1 tablespoonful celery seed, 2 stalks celery, 2 cents worth turmeric, 1½ quarts lima beans (boiled).

292

Piccalilli

1 quart lima beans (large and small), kidney or soup beans, 6 stalks celery, 4 heads cauliflower, 2 heads cabbage, peppers (red, green and yellow), 3 doz. pickles, 6 carrots, 1 quart onions, 1 quart green tomatoes, 1 quart vinegar to 1 cup of sugar, spices to taste.

293

Pennsylvania Dutch Compound Vinegar

1 pound of tarragon, 4 ounces of mustard seeds, 6 cloves of garlic, 6 small onions, 4 ounces of elder blossoms, $\frac{1}{4}$ ounce of cloves, 4 quarts of white vinegar.

Put all together to steep in a two gallon jug, corking tight and let stand several weeks before using.

294

Dutch Pickled Yellow Beans

Use only large and tender beans. After stringing, boil in salted water until tender. Drain and then pour cider vinegar over them. If the vinegar is too strong, add some water. Pack in jars or crocks.

295

Dutch Sour Beets

6 or 8 beets	1 tablespoon sugar
2 cups vinegar	1 teaspoon salt
3 hard-boiled eggs	$\frac{1}{2}$ teaspoon pepper

Boil the beets until tender, peel and slice them one-half inch thick; season. Then pour over them the vinegar and let stand for 30 minutes. Add the peeled hardboiled eggs and let lie in the vinegar for 24 hours, after which they will be colored red.

296
Dutch Pepper Cabbage

1 small head cabbage	1 tablespoon vinegar
1 stalk celery	salt, pepper
2 small peppers	

Chop the cabbage, the peppers and the celery, add the seasonings and cook until tender.

297
Dutch Sour Jerusalems

10 Jerusalem artichokes	1 cup vinegar
tablespoon butter	salt, pepper, cayenne

Boil the artichokes for 40 minutes in salted water, rinse in cold water, and let cool. Dice, and pour over them the vinegar sauce mixture.

298
Sour Cherry Pineapple Marmalade

2 quarts sour cherries	Sugar
1 pineapple	

Put the cherries through a grinder. Add juice to the ground cherries. Peel and slice the pineapple and put through grinder in same way. Make the proportions ¾ cup pineapple and juice to 1 cup cherries and juice. Add sugar equal in weight to both. Cook slowly until thick, and preserve in mason jars.

299
Dutch Pickled Oysters

1 gallon oysters	1 tablespoon allspice
1 pint vinegar	1 tablespoon black pepper
2 lemons	3 pieces mace
5 pods red pepper	

Drain a gallon of oysters; wash them in cold water and drain again. Stew them gently till their edges curl. Put oyster liquor in another pot and add one tablespoon allspice, one tablespoon whole black pepper, three pieces of mace, five small pods of red pepper and salt to taste.

Boil until liquor is nicely flavored, then add one pint of good vinegar. Add two lemons in slices, and pour the hot liquor over the hot oysters. Set away in a cold place for a day.

13

Dutch Pudding and Desserts

Desserts with the Pennsylvania Dutch were (as with the English) more likely to be a pudding than the lighter kind we modern Americans are used to. Thus we find a lot of Dutch puddings, some so simple and dull that I do not mention them, such as Graham pudding, steamed bread pudding, bread and apple pudding, sponge bread pudding, corn meal pudding, etc. These are poverty puddings, out of the thrifty colonial past.

But there are others worth mentioning, such as baked peach pudding, rhubarb pudding, steamed walnut pudding, *Gotterspeise*, Pennsylvania Plum Pudding, etc.

300
Dutch Peach Dumplings

1 cup sugar	1 cup flour
1 tablespoon butter	2 teaspoons baking powder
1 cup milk or cream	½ teaspoon salt
2 cups sliced peaches	

Make a syrup of the sugar, with the butter and 2 cups hot water. Add the peaches. Let this come to a boil. Make dumplings by mixing flour and baking powder and salt into a fairly stiff batter with milk or cream. Drop large cooking spoonfuls of this batter into the boiling syrup and peaches, cover and cook for 20 minutes. Serve sizzling hot.

301
Dutch Huckleberry Pudding

2 eggs	1 cup flour
1 cup sugar	1 teaspoon baking powder
1 cup huckleberries	

Mix the eggs and sugar, add ½ cup of cold water, the flour, sifted, mixed with baking powder. Mix with the huckleberries. Serve with milk.

302
Dutch Puffs (*Krapfen*)

(Favorites of Peter and Frederick Muhlenberg)

4 cups flour	1 oz. yeast
1½ cups butter	½ cup cream
2 tablespoons sugar	2 oranges (rind only)
½ teaspoon salt	cinnamon
6 eggs	

Set a sponge in the usual manner as for bread, but with only one cup of flour. Let rise in warm place. Spread the other 3 cups of flour on board, and place the butter, beaten eggs, cream, salt and sugar in center, work well with the hands and with knuckles, rubbing the paste rapidly toward the edges of the board, and then bringing to a heap with both hands. Lift it up and throw down on the board, with some force, for four or five minutes.

When the sponge has risen add it to the paste, working it in thoroughly. Flour a napkin, put the paste in it, and set in moderately cool place to rise for 4 hours. Then knead it on the slab, after which let it cool for 30 minutes. Cut into about 30 pieces of equal size, knead these into balls, and place on separate buttered sheets of paper. Place these, paper and all, on baking tins, to rise in warm place. Then immerse in hot Crisco or lard until golden brown. Drain and then sprinkle over them cinnamon. Also rub the orange rind on sugar and scrape off, and sprinkle this sugar on the golden brown *krapfen*.

303
Prune Dumplings (*Zwetchen Dampfnudeln*)

1 qt. bread sponge

This dish is prepared at the same time bread is baked. Regular bread sponge is made, left to rise overnight, and in the morning about a quart of the bread dough is set aside for the dumplings. Rolled into small balls of about 2 inches in diameter they are left on a floured baking board in a warm place, to rise to double their size. These dumplings are then dropped into a stew pot in which prunes have been stewed, together with some lemon peel and a few slices of apple The stew water is first brought to a boil before the dumplings are added, and they are cooked for 30 minutes, closely covered. Serve with prunes and juice.

304
Dutch Apple Sauce Cake

2 cups flour	½ cup butter
1 cup apple sauce	1 teaspoon baking soda
1 cup brown sugar	1 teaspoon cinnamon
1 cup raisins	½ teaspoon cloves
½ teaspoon salt	1 grated nutmeg

Mix butter, sugar and cloves, nutmeg, cinnamon. Mix the baking soda in the applesauce, then add the flour and applesauce to mixture. Bake in moderate oven.

305
Dutch Wine Dessert (Gotterspeise)

1 dozen ladyfingers	1 tablespoon cornstarch
6 macaroons	3 eggs
1 pint port wine	3 tablespoons sugar

Fill three-quarters full a bake dish with the ladyfingers and macaroons, cut into small pieces. Warm the wine, adding the cornstarch, eggs (only yolks) and sugar. Stir, and pour the mixture into the bakedish with cake. When cool cover with well beaten white of eggs, sprinkle with sliced almonds and bake 10 minutes in oven. Serve cold.

306
Dutch Plum Pudding

2 eggs	$\frac{1}{4}$ cup minced citron
1 cup milk	2 teaspoons baking powder
1 cup molasses	$\frac{1}{2}$ teaspoon salt
1 cup chopped beef suet	1 cup bread crumbs
1 cup raisins	1 cup flour
$\frac{1}{2}$ cup currants	$\frac{1}{2}$ cup chopped almonds

Mix all the ingredients, using flour to mold into stiff paste. Steam for 3 hours in a mold. Sprinkle the almonds over it, and serve with hard sauce.

307
Dutch Rhubarb Dumplings

12 stalks rhubarb	$1\frac{1}{2}$ teaspoons baking powder
3 cups flour	2 tablespoons brown sugar
1 cup milk	2 tablespoons butter

Skin the rhubarb, cut into inch pieces, cook (in bake pan) slowly with one cup of water and brown sugar. Then prepare batter, sifting the flour with baking powder and salt, and two tablespoons of butter, together with one egg, beaten, with milk enough added to form stiff batter. Drop kitchen spoonfuls of batter into hot stewing rhubarb. Then bake in oven for 20 minutes or so until golden brown. Serve in individual dessert dishes, with hard sauce or vanilla sauce.

308
Dutch Baked Peaches

3 cups flour	½ cup butter
2 teaspoons baking powder	1 cup milk
½ teaspoon salt	2 cups sugar

Mix the flour with baking powder and salt, then with butter, and then with milk enough to make a dough. Roll out thick, make strips to enclose whole pared fresh or canned peaches. Pinch together closely the strips encircling the peaches. Put in bake pan; make a syrup of sugar and a cup of water, brought to a boil, pour around the peaches, and bake 30 minutes in medium hot oven.

309
Dutch Cream

1½ pints milk	2 oz. gelatine
1½ pints thick cream	¾ cup maraschino
1½ cups sugar	

Set the milk over the fire with the sugar and gelatine, and stir until the gelatine is dissolved—nearly at the boiling point. Then strain it into an ice cream freezer, set in ice water, and let it get nearly cold. Whip the cream to froth; beat the milk in the freezer likewise, and then mix the two and continue beating until it is a delicate white sponge; then mix in the maraschinos while beating.

Dutch Cream may be served with compote of pears, or with grapes, white cherries or with strawberries, uncooked; the compotes, of course, to be ice cold, a spoonful served like a sauce with the white cream.

310

Dutch Sweet Sauce

Stew six ounces of dried cherries in two glasses of red wine, together with some bruised cinnamon, cloves, and lemon peel for twenty minutes on slow fire; pass the whole through a colander, into a puree, and put it into a stewpan with a little reduced brown sauce and 2 cups of stewed prunes.

311

Dutch Plum Pudding, Eschbach

2 lbs. white bread crumbs	1 lb. currants
1 lb. white sugar	1 pt. milk
1 lb. chopped suet	1 teaspoon mixed spices
7 eggs	(Cinnamon, nutmeg, mace)
½ cup brandy	1 teaspoon salt
1 lb. raisins	½ teaspoon baking soda

Mix all the dry ingredients together, grating or crumbing the bread fine. Then add the milk, eggs and brandy, with the salt and soda dissolved in them. Tie in pudding cloth and boil for four hours. Serve whole, or steamed with fancy molds.

312

Dutch Blackberry Mush

Mash 1 qt. of very ripe blackberries, sweeten to taste, cook 15 minutes, stir in flour enough to make them stick together. Keep boiling all the time. Pour into cups, when cold, eat with cream.

313

Dutch Cherry Sauce

Seed sour cherries and cover with vinegar. Let stand 24 hours and drain off vinegar. Take same quantity sugar as cherries and put first layer of cherries, then sugar, etc., and let this stand a week, stirring every day. Put in jars and seal.

314

Dutch Rice Apples

Boil $\frac{1}{2}$ lb. rice until soft, add 1 qt. sweet milk, $\frac{1}{2}$ small cup of sugar. Pare and core 7 or 8 good cooking apples, place in a buttered dish, put 1 teaspoonful jelly into each cavity, and fill with rich cream, put rice in around the apples, leaving top uncovered.

Bake 30 minutes, then cover with white of 2 eggs and sifted sugar. Brown. Serve with cream.

315

Dutch Sherry Sauce

Take a carrot, onion, and a head of celery; cut them into very small dice, and place in a stewpan with two ounces of raw lean of ham cut similarly; some thyme, and a bay-leaf, a blade of mace, a few peppercorns, and some parsley. Fry these with a little butter, of a light brown color; moisten with 1 cup of sherry and $\frac{1}{2}$ cup of vinegar; reduce the above to one half its quantity, and then add a small ladleful of brown sauce and a little consomme; stir the sauce until it boils, and then set it aside to clear itself; skin it, and pass it through a colander into a bain-marie for use.

316

Philadelphia Peach Ice Cream

1 pint chopped peaches	$\frac{1}{2}$ teaspoon lemon juice
1 pint light cream	1 cup sugar

After paring and cutting the peaches fine, pour over them the sugar and let stand for 30 minutes. Press through a colander and add the lemon juice. Then in the packed ice cream freezer combine the cream and the peaches and freeze in the usual way.

317
Dutch Apple Pudding

1 pint flour	½ teaspoon salt
2 teaspoons baking powder	1 egg
2 tablespoons butter	1 cup milk
2 tablespoons sugar	1 doz. tart apples

Sift together flour, salt and baking powder, then cream the butter, sugar, egg and milk, then add the flour mixture to make dough. Roll out a half inch thick and line a bake pan with it. Pare the apples and cut into slices and place on the dough. Sprinkle with sugar and cinnamon and cover with the remaining dough. Bake for 30 minutes.

318
Dutch Cheese Custard

5 eggs	½ cup powdered sugar
1 cup cream	2 tablespoons butter
1 cup cottage cheese	1 teaspoon grated nutmeg

Put the cheese into a bowl and stir in the cream, sugar, egg yolks, beaten, and the butter, melted, sprinkle over it the nutmeg, and fold in the stiffly beaten whites of eggs. Place pie crust in glass or earthen pie dish and pour in the custard. Bake at bottom of quick oven for 40 minutes. Serve hot.

319
Peach Short Cake, Lebanon

1 egg	3 teaspoons baking powder
1 cup milk	½ teaspoon salt
2 cups flour	¼ cup shortening
Fresh peaches	¼ teaspoon cinnamon
2 tablespoons sugar	

Sift together the flour, sugar, baking powder, salt. Blend in the shortening, mix the egg and milk and add. Stir and put into greased pan. Lay over this the peaches, pealed and halved. Sprinkle with cinnamon and bake in moderate oven.

320
Dutch Apple Snow

1 large sour apple   2 eggs
1 cup powdered sugar

Grate the apple (sprinkling the sugar over it as you grate to keep the apple from darkening). Break into the apple the whites of the eggs. Beat constantly for 30 minutes in large bowl. Serve in a glass dish surrounded with a smooth custard.

321
Raspberry Punch, Conestoga

3 qts. raspberries   Sugar
1½ pints vinegar

After washing raspberries, pour over them the vinegar and stir well. Let stand 24 hours, then mash and strain through sieve. Add 3 cups of sugar to each pint of juice. Chill and serve one half juice one half water, with mint leaves.

322
Philadelphia Pudding

6 or 8 apples	2 tablespoons butter
1 or 2 tablespoons sugar	1 teaspoon cinnamon
2 eggs	2 cups flour
1 cup cream (or milk)	2 teaspoons baking powder
½ cup raisins	

Wash and core but do not peel the apples (of the tart kind). Arrange in bake pan with plenty of space. Dot each apple with butter, sprinkle with sugar and cinnamon, and put some raisins in the cores. (If there is cider, pour some in each core). Bake until soft. Then make a batter of the egg whites, the sugar mixed with the egg yolks, the cream or milk, almost a tablespoon of butter and the flour into which the baking powder has been sifted. Pour this batter over the apples and bake until brown. Serve hot—perhaps with hard sauce.

14

Dutch Cakes, Cookies, Etc.

Like all peoples of German origins, cakes are great Dutch favorites. They made a most amazing variety of them.

First of all were the simple "coffee cakes" or "crumb cakes" which were half bread, half cake. They facilitated the "dunking" which the Dutch liked in common with so many other peoples of Mid-European origin.

The varieties of recipes available comprise far more than I am providing here. I excluded many which are known to other people, such as marble cake, ice cream cake, pound cake, etc. I also excluded some of the simpler and less attractive kinds, for the number becomes quite wearisome. I found more Dutch cake recipes than recipes for any other single division of food.

The Dutch celebrated every event with cakes of some kind or other, the climax being, of course Christmas. The baking activities of some Dutch *hausfraus* at Christmas time when the *Bells-Nickle* was abroad, is still often enormous. The German Lebkuchen, internationally famous, is also made extensively. The Dutch also pay real attention to bread. They bake many varieties, and very early made good rye bread by securing the rye flour without separation. They also baked pumpernickel, potato bread, etc.

In modern times bread consumption has been cut by all peoples, including the Dutch. In 1875 the people of the U. S. ate 1088 loaves of bread annually per family, and I do not doubt that the Dutch consumption was at least 1200 loaves per family. But this consumption of bread has been cut in half since 1875.

The hearth-baked breads of the Dutch must have tempted large consumption simply by its appeal to the nose, if not also to the eyes,—perhaps also by the wonderful dairy butter, jams, applebutter and cheese spreads available.

323
Dutch Kaffee Kuchen

1 egg	½ cup butter and lard
1 cup sugar	1 yeast cake
2 cups milk	7 cups flour

Scald milk, let cool slightly. Mix sugar, butter, lard, and egg yolk, then add to milk, alternately with flour to which yeast, dissolved has been added. Beat and then add well beaten egg white. Let rise for 2 or 3 hours. Flour a bread board, and roll out flat cakes from large spoonfuls of dough. Place in greased pie pans, let rise 1½ hours. Brush with melted butter, crumb with brown sugar or Dutch "rivels" (made of crumbed sugar, flour and butter), and bake in medium hot oven.

324
Coffee Bread

2 eggs	½ cup sugar
3 cups of flour	¼ cup butter
1 cup warm milk	1 yeast cake
½ teaspoon salt	1 cup bread crumbs
¼ cup blanched chopped almonds	2½ tablespoons brown sugar
	1 teaspoon cinnamon

Mix sugar and butter, pour warm milk over it, add yeast, dissolved. Add the eggs well beaten, flour and salt, to make a batter. Beat, and let rise for 1½ hours. Beat again, place in deep pie pans, sprinkled with flour. Make crumbing by mixing bread crumbs, brown sugar, cinnamon, ½ teaspoon salt, almonds and 2 tablespoons nearly melted butter. Mix in bowl, spread over cakes, let rise for 15 minutes and bake in medium hot oven.

325

Cinnamon Kuchen

1 yeast cake	½ teaspoon salt
½ cup butter	1 egg
¾ cup sugar	5½ cups flour

Scald a pint of milk, and when partly cooled add yeast, dissolved, and 3½ cups of flour. Beat well, let rise for 2 hours. Then cream butter and sugar, add salt, beat egg into it and add remainder of flour, enough to stiffen. Let rise for an hour. Cut into four sections, roll out each to inch thickness. Place in pie tins, let rise another hour. Then dent the top with a number of dents, brush with melted butter, sprinkle with brown sugar, sift cinnamon over it, and bake 25 to 30 minutes in medium hot oven.

326

Quaker Biscuits

3 eggs, separated	¾ cup lard and butter mixed
6 cups flour	1 yeast cake
1 pint milk	

Prepare a dough sponge of the above ingredients and set about 2½ hours to rise. Roll out thinly, cut into round biscuits, brush each with melted butter. Pile in stacks of two—one on top of another, let rise another hour. Then brush tops with yolk of an egg mixed with milk. Then bake in moderately hot oven.

327
Dutch Kisses

1 cup powdered sugar
3 eggs
½ teaspoon salt

1½ cups hickory nuts or English walnuts

Beat the whites of eggs stiffly, add the salt, sugar and then the nuts. Make teaspoon drops of this batter and bake in greased and floured pan in medium hot oven.

328
Dutch Currant Cake

2 cups sugar
1 cup butter
1 cup currants
½ teaspoon baking soda
1 teaspoon cream of tartar

4 eggs
1 cup milk
4½ cups flour
1 teaspoon cinnamon
½ teaspoon grated nutmeg

Mix butter, sugar and eggs, add nutmeg and cinnamon, then add milk and flour alternately, with flour, after sifting in cream of tartar. Dissolve baking soda in a little water, add currants, floured, and then the whites of eggs well beaten. Bake slowly in medium hot oven.

329
Schwingfelder (Potato) Cakes

1 cup potatoes mashed
½ cup lard
½ cup butter
1 yeastcake

1 teaspoon salt
3 eggs
2 cups sugar

Mix 1 cup of sugar and the hot mashed potatoes; after cooling add 1 cup flour and yeast, dissolved; beat and let rise 3 hours. Mix lard, butter 1 cup of sugar, eggs and salt; mix this with the sponge and beat vigorously, and stir stiff. Let rise overnight roll out, cut, place biscuits in pans, spread with melted butter, sift brown sugar over them. Bake 20-30 minutes in moderate oven.

330

Potato (Grumbera) Biscuit

2 potatoes	1 tablespoon butter
½ cake yeast	1 egg
3 cups flour	½ teaspoon salt
1 teaspoon sugar	

Boil and mash potatoes, dissolve yeast in water from potato boiler, mix it with 1 cup of flour and teaspoon of sugar. Let rise for 1½ hours in warm place, then add butter, egg and salt, beaten, also two cups flour; beat again and let rise for an hour. Roll to one inch thickness, and cut; then dip each biscuit in melted butter and place in pans, where let rise for another hour. Bake in hot oven and serve fresh and hot.

331

Fruit Bread — "Hutzel Brod"

2 eggs	1 yeast cake
3 cups dried pears	⅓ teaspoon baking soda
2 cups pear juice	½ cup butter
1 lb. raisins, soaked	¼ cup lard
½ teaspoon salt	1 teaspoon fennel seed
3 cups flour	2 teaspoons cinnamon
1 cup brown sugar	

Stew the dried pears gently for half hour; separate the juice, add yeast after dissolving in warm water. Mix with flour and salt, cover and let stand overnight. Then add soda dissolved in warm water. Mix lard, butter, eggs and sugar. Dice the pears, sift flour over them, add raisins, fennel and cinnamon, stiffen with flour and knead, give plenty of time to rise.

Mold into four or five loaves, brush with melted butter and bake 1 hour to 1¼ hours in moderate oven.

332

Old Dutch Molasses Cakes

1 quart molasses
2 lbs. brown sugar
2 oz. soda
1 oz. cream of tartar

1 lb. lard
1 quart sour milk
4 lbs. flour

Make the dough 12 hours before the baking. Must be very cold to roll, cut with round cutter and brush with egg before baking. Bake in slow oven.

333

Fruit Kuechen

⅓ cup sugar
⅓ cup milk
⅓ cup butter

1 egg
1 cup flour
1 teaspoon baking powder

Spread in a pan about 8½x8½ inches, then pile 1 quart of cherries, peaches, blue berries or plums mixed with 1 cup of sugar on top of the dough and bake for 40 minutes in moderate oven. Serve with whipped cream.

334

Moravian Coffee Cake

About 6 P.M. put 2 teacupfuls of warm mashed potatoes, 1 teacupful of home made yeast, and I teacupful white sugar, into a bowl to rise. About 9 P.M. mix into this 1 egg, 1 teacupful melted butter with enough flour to make a dough like that for rolls. Next morning put the dough into pans, smoothing it out with the palm of the hand, as it will be too thin to roll out. Let it rise until very light, then with your thumb make deep holes, about an inch or more apart on the surface. Into each hole put a small lump of butter, a tiny pinch of cinnamon and a generous one of light brown sugar. Bake in quick oven and eat with coffee.

335
Lebanon Rusks

1 teacup mashed potatoes, 1 cup sugar, 1 cup yeast, 4 eggs beaten separately. Stir this together and let it begin to raise at 8:30 A.M. Let raise until noon. Then add ½ cup butter and lard mixed, enough flour to make stiff. Let raise until 3 P.M. Shape into rolls and raise again. Bake in a quick oven 15 minutes.

336
Midnight Cake

2 cups brown sugar, ½ cup shortening, 2 eggs, 2 cups flour, 1 level teaspoonful of soda dissolved in ½ cup of thick milk, 2 oz. melted chocolate, 1 cup of hot coffee, 1 teaspoonful of vanilla. Beat sugar, butter and eggs together, add melted chocolate and coffee. Let cool, mix flour and last add milk and soda.

337
Hickory Nut Cake

2 cups of white sugar, 3 cups of flour, ½ cup of sweet milk, one-third cup of butter, 4 eggs, 2 teaspoonfuls baking powder, 2 cups of kernels.

338
Dutch Ginger Cakes

One-half cup of sugar, 1 cup molasses, ½ cup butter, 1 teaspoonful of cinnamon, 1 teaspoonful of ginger, ¾ teaspoonful of cloves, 2 even teaspoonfuls of soda in a cup of hot water, 2½ cups of flour, 2 well beaten eggs. Bake in muffin rings in a quick oven.

339

Onion Cake

Take curd and mix with good rich milk to the consistency of cottage cheese. Fry sliced onions until soft in butter and add to cheese. Season with salt; bake in pastry.

340

Tangled Jackets

1 pint of sour milk, 3 eggs, ½ teaspoonful soda, 1 teaspoonful salt, 1 pound flour. Mix and cook in deep fat.

341

Dutch Fat Cakes

1 lb. sugar, ¼ lb. butter, 4 eggs, 1 cup sweet milk, 1 teaspoonful soda, and flour to stiffen. Drop in deep fat.

342

Dutch Puff Ball Doughnuts

3 eggs, 1 cup of sugar, 3 cups of milk, ½ teaspoonful of salt, ½ teaspoonful of nutmeg, 2 teaspoonfuls of baking powder, about 1 qt. of flour. Mix and drop by spoonfuls into deep fat.

343

Dutch Doughnuts

Boil and mash 3 or 4 large potatoes in water enough to make 3 cups. To this add ¼ teaspoon salt, 1 cup of yeast (or 1 cake dissolved), 1 cup of sugar, ½ cup of lard, enough flour to make a stiff batter. Cover well, keep in warm place over night. In the morning add 2 eggs, work into a soft dough, let rise, cut into cakes, let rise again, bake in deep fat.

344

Dutch Snowballs

Take 2 eggs, and ½ cup of sweet milk, add flour enough to make a stiff dough, also a little salt. Roll thin and cut into four-inch squares. Have ready a pan of deep fat. Mark each square with a knife into strips ½ inch wide, but leaving a border of half an inch. Pick them up to place in lard when hot, by taking alternate strips and lay them in sideways. They puff up into a flaky ball, and make a very nice addition to lunch or tea.

345

Dutch Crullers

2 eggs, 1 cup sugar, 1 pint of thick milk, ¼ pint of butter and lard mixed, 1 teaspoonful of soda and ½ teaspoonful of cream of tartar dissolved in the milk. Flavor with nutmeg and add flour sufficient to roll. Swim in hot fat.

346

Dutch Cakes (*Schneckenhaus'ln*)

Dissolve a yeast cake in ¼ cup of lukewarm water. Add 1 tablespoonful of sugar, a little salt, and flour to stiffen to a sponge. Let rise about 1 hour. Now add 2 cups of lukewarm milk, 4 tablespoonfuls of sugar, ½ cup of melted butter, (butter and lard will do) 2 eggs beaten whole, 1 qt. of sifted flour enough to make a soft sponge. Let rise again. Roll out, spread with a mixture of butter, sugar, and cinnamon, cut into strips and roll up from one end. Place in pans and let rise a third time, then bake in a quick oven.

347

Dutch Molasses Crumb Cake

2 cups brown sugar	¾ cup New Orleans molasses
1 cup butter and lard mixed	1 cup hot water
3 cups flour	1 teaspoonful of soda

Mix sugar, flour and butter together, using the hands to make into crumbs. Put molasses into separate vessel, and into it stir the soda and hot water. Put soda into cup and dissolve with a little water, before filling the cup to the full. Put pastry into deep pans, pour in the molasses mixture, and sprinkle the crumbs over the top, and bake at once in a moderate oven.

348
Lady Lancaster Cake

1 cup butter	For filling:
2 cups sugar	3 cups granulated sugar
6 egg whites	3 egg whites
1 cup milk	$\frac{1}{2}$ teaspoon vanilla flavor
3$\frac{1}{2}$ cups flour	$\frac{1}{2}$ cup chopped raisins
2 teaspoons baking powder	1 cup chopped nuts
1 teaspoon vanilla	5 figs, cut in thin strips

Cream the butter and sugar, add the milk and flavoring, and then the sifted flour into which the baking powder has been sifted. Then fold in the egg whites. Bake in three layer pans in a hot oven.

The filling is made by dissolving the sugar in a cup of boiling water, and cook until it "threads." Then pour it gradually over the stiffly beaten egg whites and add the flavoring, nuts, raisins and figs. Some of the fruit may be reserved for the top of the cake.

349
Popcorn Cake Mennonite

3 quarts popped corn	2$\frac{1}{2}$ cups powdered sugar
2$\frac{1}{2}$ cups chopped nuts	3 tablespoons butter

Mix the popped corn and the nuts, and then pour over it the following syrup: cook together the sugar and butter until it forms a taffy when you test it in water. Mix the syrup well with the popcorn and nuts, using a large spoon. Then butter a bake pan and put in a layer of the mixture, then press together; then another layer and press, until the dish is full. Then you can slice the "cake."

350
Fasnacht Kucha, Kutztown

1½ quarts milk	2 cakes yeast
½ cup molasses or honey	1 cup butter
4 quarts flour	4 eggs
2 tablespoons lard	

Scald the milk, then after cooling a little stir in 2 quarts of the flour, to make a batter. Add the yeast after dissolving in lukewarm water. Beat well and let stand overnight, to rise. Cream the butter; eggs, molasses or honey, and then add more flour and the lard. Knead well, adding almost all the remainder of the flour. Let rise and then roll out for doughnuts, and fry in deep fat.

351
Blitz Kucha, Ephrata

2 eggs	1½ teaspoons baking powder
1 cup sugar	¼ cup black walnuts, chopped
4 tablespoons butter	1 teaspoon vanilla
1⅓ cups flour	¼ teaspoon salt
½ cup milk	½ teaspoon cinnamon

Cream the sugar and butter, blend with the eggs, beaten. Sift together the flour, baking powder and salt, and then add alternately the milk and the vanilla. Pour into a bake pan, sprinkle with the cinnamon and the sugar and the chopped walnuts. Bake for 30 minutes in moderate oven.

352
Dutch Black Walnut Christmas Cake

2 cups sugar	1 cup milk
1 cup butter	3⅓ cups flour
5 eggs	4 teaspoons baking powder
1 pt. chopped black walnut meats	⅓ teaspoon salt

Cream the butter and then work in the eggs (well-beaten) and sugar. Then sift the flour, baking powder and salt; add the nuts and stir alternately into the first mixture together with the milk. Oil a large cake pan put in the mixture and bake for 50 minutes in moderate oven. Spread a nut icing over it.

353

Dutch "Shell Bark" Macaroons

⅓ cup brown sugar
1 cup hickory nut meat, chopped
⅓ cup granulated sugar

2 eggs
½ teaspoon baking powder
1 teaspoon milk
¼ teaspoon salt

After beating the eggs, mix in the sugar and other ingredients, first the brown then white sugar, then the flour, baking powder, milk, salt, and finally the nuts. Roll the mixture out to one half-inch thickness, cut into macaroon size, and bake on buttered pans for 15 minutes in moderate oven.

354

Oat Meal Cakes, Drexel

3 cups oatmeal
2 cups flour
1 cup butter and lard
1 cup raisins
2 cups sugar

1 teaspoon cinnamon
1 teaspoon baking soda
¼ cup milk
2 eggs

Sift flour and baking soda together and mix with all other ingredients except eggs and milk. Beat the eggs well and add the milk. Roll and cut into cakes and bake in moderate oven.

355

Cocoanut Crackers, Dunker

(*Modern name cocoanut snaps*)

2½ lbs. sugar
1 pt. New Orleans molasses
6 oz. butter
1½ lbs. flour

1 large cocoanut freshly
  grated
1 teaspoon baking soda

Mix well to form stiff batter. Cut in cookie form on greased baking sheets in baking pans. Bake in hot oven until brown, then remove from oven and allow to cool thoroughly without removing from pan.

356

Chocolate Cookies, Adventist

1 cup New Orleans molasses
2 cups brown sugar
1 cup grated Bakers chocolate (3 squares)

1 cup butter
1 teaspoon baking soda
Flour

Mix the ingredients to make a stiff batter, using just flour enough to roll. Cut out with a cookie cutter about 1½ inches in diameter. Bake the cookies in a hot oven, on greased paper. Then when baked and cooled, put in a stone crock in a cool place and *keep for a month or six weeks before eating.* (The early Dutch baked them at Thanksgiving time for Christmas use). The result is a soft, chewy cookie with a caramel effect which men particularly like.

357

Dutch "Shellbark" and Raisin Cake

5 eggs
¾ cup butter
2 cups sugar
1 cup raisins

1 cup milk
3 cups flour
2 teaspoons baking powder
1 cup hickory-nut meats

Mix all the ingredients, add the stiffly beaten whites of the eggs, and bake in layers. Ice with vanilla icing.

358
Dutch Coffee Fruit Cake

½ lb. butter
2 cups brown sugar
2 tablespoons molasses
1 grated nutmeg
3 cups currants
1 teaspoon baking powder

1 teaspoon allspice
1 egg
1 teaspoon cinnamon
flour
½ pint warm coffee

Cream the butter, add the sugar. Dissolve the baking powder in the molasses, add to mixture, and then mix in the allspice, the egg, beaten, the cinnamon and nutmeg. Add the coffee to the mixture and mix in flour to make batter, and then add the currants which have been floured. Pour into greased pans and bake 2½ or 3 hours in moderate oven.

15

Around the Food Season with my Grandmother at the Farm

To fully appreciate my tale of my grandmother's remarkably extensive food skills (which thousands of other Dutch grandmothers of ten generations could equal, and do equal in some Dutch regions even today), you will need to realize several facts.

First of all, you will need to realize that America was developed on this economic principle: *the principle of self-sustaining farms,* which purchased almost nothing and manufactured almost everything it needed. Thus the colonists created the wealth of America.

Second, you will need to realize that the Pennsylvania Dutch were almost from the very first (unlike most other early American colonists) a farm people; a very versatile and skilled people, and above all a quite exceptionally industrious and thrifty people.

Third, you will need to realize that the Dutch were never content to be only self-sustaining—they brought their section of America up to farming prosperity and fertility faster than the people of any other section in America—*by becoming particularly active farm producers and sellers of surplus.* The Lancaster County Dutch carried their surplus as much as fifty miles to market over rough colonial trails, in their great Conestoga wagons. As nowhere else in America therefore the Dutch developed *farm market-places,* which are even today unique sights and characteristics of such cities as Philadelphia, Lancaster, Reading, etc. These are street stands where farmers sell from their wagons, or large market buildings where the farmers have stalls.

Fourth, you will need to realize that the Dutch farm housewife was a vital if not dominating part of this plan of farm production and marketing farm surplus. She became a master of a phenomenally wide range of food manufacturing arts; and furthermore she went personally to market in the market-wagons, to meet her customers face-to-face, and to insure that her food products reached the consumer fresh, clean and pure. Thus the Dutch farm family reaped all the profits, both of manufacture, transportation, wholesaling and distribution. That is how they prospered, and prosper today; that indeed is why even the depression has not seriously harmed the Dutch families still engaged in this early colonial farm economics.

With these points in mind, my story of my grandmother's farm food activities will be more than a personal recollection; it will be the story, the saga of the Pennsylvania Dutch and their unique economic basis; which also is in lesser degree the story of all colonial farm economics. The Dutch carried this economic principal further and kept at it until a later date than most other groups. It will also disclose the secret of why the Pennsylvania Dutch housewife became so superbly skilled with food.

As a young boy, visiting my grandparent's farm along the

banks of the Tulpehocken near Reading I could see this saga of Dutch life with particular vividness, because there were still standing the original log-cabin barns and out-buildings, thatched with straw in European style, which were erected when these Dutch first came to America almost a century before the Revolution. I could see my grandfather make his own shoes, forge his own iron in his own smithy, and grind his own corn. I could see all the other activities which have now really disappeared and which in other parts of America had disappeared fifty or a hundred years before the Dutch dropped them. I was thus able to see a fair part of colonial civilization still operating as late as 1888.

From the first my grandmother's genius with food astounded and fascinated me. In her long lifetime of 88 years her hands were never still and no conjurer ever pulled rabbits out of a hat with the facility that she exercised with food from May until December, in preparing and producing an endless variety of things to eat. It is probably literally true that if all the food she produced in her lifetime could be piled in one heap, it would be taller than the tallest Egyptian pyramid! She produced food of course not only for her family and the farm-hands, but wagon-loads of it to sell each week, winter and summer, in the city farm market-place. Rising at four she would go to the city with grandfather to sell what she had made.

I rarely saw my grandmother buy anything at a grocery store except sugar, salt, pepper, coffee, and a few other things. She usually even made her own baking powder, (there is an old Dutch recipe for it), and certainly she never deigned to buy even *tea,* for she gathered pennyroyal, mint and other herbs in the summer, dried them and they made very good tea indeed. Grandfather, by the way, never even bought matches, for after reading the weekly newspaper he cut it into six-inch squares and rolled them into tapers which were placed in a wall receptacle.

Even kerosene was a quite unnecessary concession to modernity, for grandmother made tallow candles in her own candle mold, inherited from her grandmother. And if candles failed, there was still the old *schmutz amschel* (grease lamp) made in the farm smithy, as were so many things, including copper pots and utensils. On some farms which had clay, even earthen pots and crocks for dairy use and *poi schuessel* (earthen pie plates) were baked.

So, before my grandmother began her work preparing food, when the first food harbingers of spring appeared, she and my grandfather had during the winter prepared for it by making tools and utensils. When April came the garden was prepared— and Dutch gardens are no kitchen gardens; they are usually market gardens. Great bundles of spring onions, lettuce, dandelion, were carried to town to sell, my grandmother in her neat black sunbonnet (so characteristic of these peoples) seeing personally her customers and chatting with them in no commercial vein at all.

There were 12 cows providing milk, requiring milking twice a day, and considerable volume of milk was placed in hundreds of gallon size earthen crocks at the bottom of the *"arch"* (a 20 foot-deep earthen dugout, cool even in the hottest summer). My grandmother herself skimmed all the cream from these crocks (cream separators in the eighties and nineties being unknown luxuries). Then the cream was put in a wooden barrel butter churner, cleaned as only a Dutch hausfrau can clean, and my task would be to churn it. That lovely moment when the paddles inside the barrel would begin to move stiffly as butter formed; and that lovely smell of sweet cream separating into butter and buttermilk, is still an unmatchable perfume in my memory.

My grandmother now made *schmier kase* (cottage cheese), and also Dutch cheese balls, and *sieger-kase*. When the whey separated from the curd, she proceeded next to make from this whey *cup cheese*, another typical Pennsylvania Dutch dairy product, and one of which I am particularly fond. It is apparently a delicate art to make cup cheese, and but one in six who attempt it evidently succeed, from my gourmet point of view. I do not find it often of the right consistency. My grandmother seemed to have the knack. Her *cup cheese* was never pasty and lumpy— it was always of an even, resilient consistency—a fresh, soft *gruyere* type of cheese which the French and the Swiss have made (on a factory basis) into an epicurean variety of cheese widely sold in America; one that Clemenceau, to his last day on earth, prized best. Not everybody likes this Pennsylvania *cup cheese* (so called because it is poured when liquid into white handleless china cups and is carried in cups to market, and emptied from them for each customer). Reading butter pretzels and Berks County cup cheese make a "snack" of first-class gourmet appeal.

The dandelion time in spring was not only a time for picking the green for the market; it was a time also to eat it with another Pennsylvania Dutch delicacy—hot salad dressing (see index). The very thought of dandelions served with this dressing starts salivary anticipations in me to this day!

But the ingenious Dutch had another use still for dandelion —they made dandelion wine, than which there is nothing in the line of wines with a lovelier bouquet. My grandmother expertly transforming to wine a mass of these golden blossoms was a sight to remember.

Soon, after dandelion, came the early summer fruits—raspberries and blackberries. I have the most pleasant of boyhood memories of mornings, when I followed the farm fence lines and the edges of the woods, stone piles, etc., picking these berries while the dew was still upon them, with the Dutch hills (foothills of the Alleghenies) still a little rosy with dawn.

With these berries my grandmother began—even before Spring was quite gone—the squirrel-like work of storing for the next winter's food (and also to sell in the market). She sold some berries; others she made into gorgeous pies, and still others she made into wine. But she also *dried* considerable quantities of them.

Right here it may be well to introduce that greatest of my grandmother's aids, the most potent of all instruments of Pennsylvania food delight—*the Dutch oven*. Practically every Dutch homestead, from earliest times onward, had such an oven; and they had one that differed from those of most others. It was not as a rule a fireplace oven, operatable from the kitchen fireplace. It was an outdoor oven, a separate stone structure, all whitewashed and clean; the door breast-high. With its magic aid my grandmother could do an astonishing number of things. It was my boyhood task to fire this oven. Several armfuls of brushwood, as much as the seven-foot long and two-foot high domed oven could hold, was the fuel. By the time this had been reduced to ashes—and with a long scraper I had raked them out through the iron door—the oven was ready and my grandmother was ready too. Quickly we would push in, to bake upon the bare hearth at one baking, as many as a dozen loaves of bread, seven or eight pies, five or six crumb cakes, and often also some cookies. If there had been a bit of pie-crust left over, this too was rolled out and placed on the hearth as a little special reward for me! Clang! The iron gate shut, and nature did the rest.

Certainly no authorities disagree on the point that wood fire hearth baking is the supreme cookery tool. Even in New York (to please our East side population which really demands good bread) there is hearth baking done. It puts to shame the factory gas or electric ovens, or pan bakery even in private homes. When as a boy I opened that Dutch oven door I was greeted with a perfume such as is seldom offered to modern man. There was the indescribable smell of thick bread crust browned on hot brick; the fragrance of pies and their varied content, the softer perfume of cake or cookies—all entwined together as I stood on the greensward before the oven and lifted my delighted boyish head to heaven in praise. And the eating was the best of all, with the fine grains of wood ashes imbedded in the bottom of the bread-loaves. Getting those pies, loaves and cakes out of the oven on the six foot tool with a broad flat end, took a skill which I was eager to master. Few tragedies in my life have had quite the poignancy of seeing once a large juicy huckleberry pie tumble off and crash to the ground, because of my lack of skill!

After the baked goodies were set away, my thrifty Dutch grandmother was by no means finished with that still hot oven. No Chicago packer, utilizing everything but the squeak of a pig, was more competent in conserving every resource than the Pennsylvania Dutch! My grandmother had ready for the oven large wooden trays on which were the raspberries I had picked that morning.

It was the facility of the Dutch oven that made the Pennsylvania Dutch so constantly dehydrate fruits (nowadays rarely obtainable without sulphur used in drying). Those long wooden trays, at every week's baking during the summer days, carried into the oven some fruit or other to dehydrate for the winter. Raspberries, blackberries, elderberries, huckleberries, cherries, peaches, pears, apples, plums, and many other things went into the oven and came out very good fodder indeed for the long winter.

The dried apple or pear was in particular a basis for much Pennsylvania Dutch cookery. *Schnitz and knepp* is one of the most famous of such dishes; known intimately to the Dutch for centuries. It is a luscious dumpling cooked with dried apples or pears. The idea to us moderns sounds not at all attractive —sounds even poverty-stricken and uninteresting. Many gourmets told about it raise their eyebrows. Such a plebian dish a delight? How come? To eat it is very much more delightful that to describe it; the extraordinarily good flavor of some of the apples or pears which the Pennsylvania Dutch have almost alone, cultivated (such as for instance the incomparable Smokehouse apple) accounts for the toothsomeness of this drearysounding tid-bit. The Dutch oven method of slow-drying the fruit, without paring its skin, accounts for still more. The dried apple available commercially today is indeed a poverty food; but not so the Pennsylvania Dutch *schnitz*. The *knepp* also bears study, for it was a dumpling quite unlike the soggy things one usually encounters.

The Dutch have always had good fruit orchards and their territory is propitious for apples. They used in winter the dried apple for another delicacy not likely to intrigue gourmets by mere description—the *schnitz pie;* that is to say a pie of dried apples or pears. When you have nearly six months of absence of fresh fruit, as did the Dutch for centuries, a *schnitz pie* in winter is sure to have a welcome. Nowadays we in New York or elsewhere are dreadfully spoiled; we almost ignore the seasons, since Texas, Florida, California and even Africa and Argentine dump fruits and vegetables upon us the year around. In colonial times all was very, very different. The *schnitz pie* was eaten with great relish by the Revolutionary soldiers at Valley Forge, and doubtless by Washington himself there, for he had a Dutch cook and openly expressed fondness for Dutch cookery.

Perhaps it was also because of the handiness and spaciousness of the Dutch oven that the Pennsylvania Dutch baked so many and so varied things. True, the Germans are all great eaters of bread and cake and pies; but it was a real temptation for my grandmother to load up the oven to its capacity. After all, she never had to spend a penny for flour. Up in her garret were two large wooden chests, each compartmented. There were wheat, rye, barley, graham and buckwheat flours, cornmeal and other cereals. Grandfather raised these cereals and simply loaded up a wagon with bags of them and hauled them to the nearest mill, where he made the traditional exchange of one-half in milled flours. I usually rode along on these trips and marveled at the old mill and its great water-wheel, and at the flour-covered workers.

So grandmother was not very pinching in her baking; and again following both New England, as well as Pennsylvania

Dutch tradition, we often had pie for breakfast. In fact, a choice of two or three kinds of pie!

But let me return to my round-the-season tale of my grandmother's food preparations. The first apples of the season (another peculiarly Dutch variety) was, I recall, Maiden's Blush; a name which in a boy of eight or nine was sure to set going rudimentary romance. But I was not allowed to eat any of those toothsome apples except the poorest "falls" because they were very marketable. I can still see a heaping half-peck measure of these delectable, demurely rosy-cheeked apples being sold to one of grandmother's market customers while I looked sadly on; and I can also remember being roundly scolded for stealing one!

Grandmother, as May and June came, was very busy with the garden, and then as haying time and harvest time came was doubly busy feeding the farm hands. The farm activity began then to mount to its August, September, October climax. The oven was going merrily all the time, drying cherries, gooseberries, blueberries, wild cherries, currants, apples, pears, peaches, blackberries, etc. Grandmother also made elderberry wine, wild cherry wine, blackberry wine, and preserves and pickles of all kinds.

Perhaps here it is time to mention the rather poetic traditional standard of Pennsylvania Dutch hospitality—that to make a "company" table groan properly with heartiness, there must be *"Seven sweets and seven sours."* The Pennsylvania Dutch women have been astounding masters of the art of preserves, both sweet and sour. My grandmother's cellar was a vast storehouse of "jars." They made sweets and sours to sell as well as to eat, and a bewildering variety was always to be had. As is the case with Hungarian cuisine and to a lesser extent with German, Jewish and Scandinavian cuisine, the Pennsylvania Dutch cuisine has always insisted that a dinner is quite incomplete—indeed any meal where meat in any form is served—without several kinds of sours and preserves. I have always contended that this is dietetically very sound, and my own digestion has amply seconded the notion! The Pennsylvania Dutch *chow chow* is especially a favorite! and I have always noticed that the Dutch "sours" are never so sour as to produce a chemically repelling sensation, as is so often the case with sours met with elsewhere.

Grandmother's kitchen, every day from June to December, was a continuous food factory. The berry season gave way to the tree fruit season, cherries, plums, pears, peaches, etc., and this continued until the apples were in full cry, and then came the applebutter time (lotwaerick, the Dutch call it). They have a special love of applebutter, and made huge quantities of it superlatively well. In the farm "summer house" was a fireplace, and in it hung on a crane a huge copper kettle, three feet across and almost as deep. My task was to keep the fire going, also to stir with the long stirrer the great kettle in which the applebutter was being cooked. Great batches of peeled apples and gallons and gallons of cider were the raw materials. The final product was a purple-black mass, the consistency of stiff apple sauce, and it was put away in earthen crocks of a gallon capacity each. When I see applebutter sold in glass bottles today I spurn it as effete; and I have not tasted applebutter made in any factory that can equal the Dutch farm product. As a bread spread it is equalled only by grapebutter, which my grandmother of course also made. Two healthier, tastier preserves or spreads could not possibly be devised. Perhaps the goodness of Pennsylvania Dutch applebutter is due to the various species of apples which they have developed—the Maiden Blush and Smokehouse, I have mentioned; also the Rambo, Bellflower, York Imperial and Vandevere, Mama Beam, Fanny, Winter Banana, Hiester, Susan's Spice, Evening Party, Blue Mountain, Fallowater, Smith's Cider, etc. No apple of the Northwest, too dry and flavorless, can compare with these, except perhaps in keeping quality. The Dutch applebutter has astounding keeping qualities. There was in the Lancaster Museum in 1828 a pot of applebutter made during the Revolution and still good to eat!

In the early Fall there are more wines to make, to store alongside the dandelion wine—elderberry wine (to which medical properties are ascribed, as to dandelion wine also), and wild plum, wild cherry, and wine of white clover. And wine from purple fox grapes, and white grapes. All these wines my grandmother labored over with meticulous care, bottling them in every and any kind of bottle, tall or squat, large or small—deriving her supply, I am bound to admit, from the family's plentiful patronage of patent medicines (as was so general in those days).

Simultaneous with this, cider-time. Cider was used in cooking applebutter, and it was preserved for selling, and also held in barrels until it became vinegar.

Swiftly following this came sauerkraut time, and this item has always been one of the German peoples' most useful food (as well as we know by research, also the most efficacious, with its regulatory and vitamin values). What seemed to me, a boy, quite vast quantities were made. Huge *stenners*, open headed barrels, were filled with it, and as always I was a participator. I shredded the cabbage on a big shredding board, and then I helped "stomp" it down, using for the purpose a heavy mallet-like "stomper," with a long handle. It was good muscle-making for a young lad! In olden, more primitive days in Europe, people "stomped" it down in large barrels *with their feet,* as in olden days also they did wine grapes. In endless variety of combinations during the winter we enjoyed sauerkraut—with dumplings, with meat, etc. Those people who nowadays look down on sauerkraut are simply the victims of poor messes which are served up in its name, even at modern restaurants. For its true flavor it seems to take a good German cook.

Sauerkraut-time over, my grandmother met the next food period, the storing of winter vegetables—beets, turnips, potatoes, etc. The Dutch are a potato-loving people, and why not, when they can cook them so well—as in their unique fried potatoes, and particularly in their hot potato salad, a dish which is beyond praise, and apparently unknown to vast numbers of other than Dutchmen in America. The Pennsylvania Dutch put potatoes into bread; they make even potato pretzels, potato pancakes, potato fritters, and potato this and that in rich variety. They also made a potato soup, of which I was very fond when a boy (see index).

The turnip is another winter vegetable, despised of many, but raised to glory by the Dutch. The Jerusalem artichoke is another tuber vegetable, which comes to its own among the Dutch. When pickled or any way, this artichoke puts its French brother to shame, in tastiness, as well as in substance. I cannot understand why I do not meet this excellent vegetable elsewhere very often.

By this time the sweet corn was also ripe, and then my grandmother (assisted by me and the magic Dutch oven) prepared one more of the distinctly great Pennsylvania Dutch food achievements—*Shaker dried corn.* This is another item which it seems astonishing to me that the rest of the country does not know. Shaker dried corn is corn cut from the cob and dehydrated in the Dutch oven so that it becomes as hard as dried peas. Then when it is softened in lukewarm water overnight and cooked, all the original flavor comes out in a manner which makes all canned corn seem fit only for pigs. I honestly believe that the taste of Shaker dried corn is better than the taste of corn when it is fresh from the cob! The drying process parches it slightly, and this has always improved corn flavor. All over Eastern Pennsylvania, Shaker dried corn (called Shaker I suppose because the Shaker branch of the Pennsylvania Dutch originated it) is used widely. Since it is so easily packageable I have never understood why it wasn't marketed nationally. Probably it is because the Dutch are not national minded, and it is, at its best, a farm product. Also perhaps because careless housewives prefer to open cans rather than go to the trouble of soaking the corn overnight. The Pennsylvania Dutch do things with this corn nobody else does—combining it with noodles, for example, in a tasty dish; or with chestnuts. The Dutch, by the way, also specialize on raising very good pop-corn.

My grandmother, all during August and September had of

course been making various "sours" out of green tomatoes, cucumbers, onions, peppers, pickles and vegetables, and has also made her own home-made catsup. Also she had been spicing watermelon rind, pickling beets, etc. Also she had been at work on unique "sweets" such as pear or quince *marmalade*, using Kieffer pears; also spiced Bartlett pears, ginger pears, quince honey, (of heavenly memory!) cherry marmalade, rhubarb jam, and rhubarb marmalade, lemon honey, cherry relish—as well, of course, as other standard preserves such as all the rest of the world knows.

Chestnuts and other nuts now ripening, my grandmother tackled her next task. The chestnut blight has in the last twenty years removed many of these trees, which were particularly plentiful in eastern Pennsylvania, but they still exist. My grandmother shelled them and dried them in the magic Dutch oven, and they made many tasty dishes during the winter; particularly stuffing for fowls. The Dutch country is also famed for its black walnuts (the limestone soil being particularly good for them), and these rich nuts make marvelous cookies, for instance, *Blitzkuchen*, (see index); and were also pickled. Hickory nuts, locally called *shell-barks*, were also delightful for cookies and candies. Storing these was another of grandma's food-factory jobs.

The frost was also by this time upon the pumpkin—but not upon some favored ones of my grandmother's! Weeks before she had perpetrated a little Dutch trick with some selected pumpkins which had for generations helped win the prize at the famous county fairs. She had cut the selected pumpkins off the vine, leaving an 18 inch vinetail on the pumpkin, and then put this vine-tail *in a jar of milk!* As if they were babies she tended these pumpkins, in the summer house, and by and by she had great pumpkins which delighted her market customers, and were cut into hob-goblins for the children on hollowe'en. Other pumpkins had different fates—she made them into Dutch pumpkin pies, such as I have never elsewhere encountered.

Soon now the most remarkable of all my grandmother's **food** activities began; the *butchering and meat-packing*. It is quite astounding to realize the breadth of these activities, for the great meat packers of Chicago had not much greater range of activities, nor utilized so many by-products! Butchering time usually arrived early in December, and the men of the family became part of the food factory. Together they killed, dressed and processed pigs, steers, sheep and poultry. One farm family, often without any other helpers, killed five pigs, two steers, a couple of sheep, and turkeys, geese, etc. Sometimes a complete butchering operation would be accomplished between four in the morning and eight at night! As may readily be imagined, this turned the farm home into a packing house with a vengeance! The men did the killing and dressing, and the women did most of the rest. They used another little building accessory, as useful as the Dutch oven—a "smokehouse." With especially selected woods, according to varying local tradition (and old-world wisdom from ancestral Westphalian regions) they smoked hams, sausages, tongues, bacon, pork and beef. I can still summon the rich smell of the old smokehouse, built of stone, with its blackened interior, redolent of a whole barrage of smells, mixed with the smell of woods of various fragrances, and the layers of old soot. There isn't a smell like it in the world.

With meat grinders, large mixing bowls and sausage stuffing machines, my grandparents would produce, before my astounded young eyes, a wide variety of foods; fresh pork sausage, smoked beef and beef sausages, Lebanon style bologna, highly spiced, liverwurst and half a dozen other wursts. They would smoke hams and slabs of bacon, tongues and other pieces of meat, and also render lard, which of course they used widely in cookery. These Pennsylvania Dutch women did not flinch at their job of handling the freshly killed animals; they had centuries of experience from childhood. They made meat jellies and pigs-feet jelly (a most delightful dish).

Only in a Pennsylvania Dutch territory have I ever eaten the fresh pork sausages in the style they made, or the smoked beef sausages. The Lebanon bologna, five inches in diameter, is probably over-spiced for most tastes, but it surely is appetizing. As for the hams, they were superbly flavored, never "quick-smoked" or sugar-cured. I do not think the Pennsylvania Dutch are well advised in eating their ham fried so invariably, as it toughens too easily under this treatment, but when broiled or baked or cooked I do not think their hams are often surpassed. True, their bacon, not being so thoroughly corn-fed as selected western bacon, is not top-grade, but it is tasty.

Now, also my grandmother made that masterpiece of all Pennsylvania Dutch foods, *scrapple;* known and sold throughout a fair portion of the country, and even abroad; acclaimed by epicures as an authentic item of good food. Scrapple (local name *Ponhaus*) contains delicate pork portions, cornmeal, sage and other spices, cooked and cooled in pans. To prepare it for the table you simply cut into flat squares and broil or fry it. It is made usually at "butchering time" and keeps well. A variation in scrapple is *oatmeal scrapple;* the difference being that oatmeal is used instead of cornmeal. Another slightly similar food called *Potwurst* is made at the same time, from the hearts, livers and other organs, and is packed in earthen crocks. It is more fatty than scrapple, but tasty and rich in vitamins when intelligently handled.

Once the butchering time is over, Christmas is close by and cookie and cake baking time arrives and fowl preparation. It was only after Christmas and the New Year that my grandmother ceased her seven months' continuous food-processing. From January to May she was mainly a cook, although she of course still made cheese and butter to sell throughout the Winter.

The Pennsylvania Dutch for centuries have made (like the Irish) a feast out of a funeral. Doubtless it originated in the days when these country folk were much more isolated than today and needed some event like a funeral to make a major social occasion. And of course it necessitated much attention to food, for the relatives and friends traveled on vehicles and horseback from many miles' distance.

When one of my grandmother's sisters died the first thing I noted was that two days before the funeral a dozen women of the family converged upon the farm from afar, bringing dishes, pots and often provisions. They began a two-day food preparation on a large scale; usually insisting that the women of the bereaved family do no work. The cooking and baking was vast and continuous. Then on the funeral day, the burial was in the morning, and the table was set for as many people as could possibly be seated at one time. The meal began at noon, and as fast as one group finished, another group sat down. At 6 P.M. there were often still people at the table; those having the longest journey back home usually, by tradition, sitting down first.

That dining table was loaded to the gunwales with every possible variety of food; and of course the traditional "seven sweets and seven sours" were there in abundance. So was "funeral pie," as the dried sour cherry pie or raisin pie came to be called, since it was so often the best pie that could be made if the funeral came in the period of December to May. "There will be raisin pie soon" was always an ominous phrase with the Dutch, meaning that death was imminent.

What I marveled at, as a boy seeing this scene (now almost extinct in our era of good roads and automobiles and movies), was the distinctly social character of the funeral occasion. The grief and sorrow was not visible; that was for privacy and at the church and graveyard. Indeed, the matter-of-fact manner of these mourners' discussion of the deceased one's grave clothes and coffin countenance was very bewildering to me—until in later years I read of the quite similar attitude which the Greeks had toward death, as is illustrated on the tombstones in the cemetery at the foot of the Acropolis. No tears or tearing of hair at death; it is taken as natural as birth. My grandmother,

15 years ahead of her death, sewed her shroud, chose her coffin and her burial rites and hymns.

In older days, a somewhat similar conclave, with great feasting, was held on the occasion of a wedding, or when a Pennsylvania Dutch farmer moved from one farm to another. Neighbors, relatives and friends would come at moving time with their biggest farm wagons and helped transport the many possessions to the new homestead. Usually the wagons proceeded soon after dawn in procession formation, the moving farmer leading the way, and the drivers in hilarious possession of a demijohn of liquor.

The women had several days before gone to the new homestead and begun the food preparations, culminating in the feast when the caravan of wagons arrived. Perhaps it is now clearer to the reader why I could say that a Dutch woman of 88 years of age could boast of having, in her lifetime, prepared a pyramid of food as high as the greatest Egyptian pyramid of Rameses! No wonder Prof. Weygandt tells of a Dutch woman who asked "how can a woman be happy with less than seven people to cook for?" Also of the little Dutch girl who replied, when asked why she was so fat, "because I have free helps of everysing." (An answer which discloses some of the notorious humor of the Dutch person who is not yet rid of "Dutchisms") .

Possibly after finishing the reading of this tale of the march of the seasons with my grandmother, food manufacturer extraordinary, the reader of this book will have a fair inkling of the backgrounds of Pennsylvania Dutch cookery, and the enormous range of a Dutch farm wife's food preparation.

Index to Recipes

The numbers attached to these receipes refer to the recipe numbers printed with each recipe in this book.
They do NOT refer to PAGE numbers.

A CATALOG OF SELECTED
DOVER BOOKS
IN ALL FIELDS OF INTEREST

A CATALOG OF SELECTED DOVER
BOOKS IN ALL FIELDS OF INTEREST

CONCERNING THE SPIRITUAL IN ART, Wassily Kandinsky. Pioneering work by father of abstract art. Thoughts on color theory, nature of art. Analysis of earlier masters. 12 illustrations. 80pp. of text. 5⅜ × 8½.   23411-8 Pa. $3.95

ANIMALS: 1,419 Copyright-Free Illustrations of Mammals, Birds, Fish, Insects, etc., Jim Harter (ed.). Clear wood engravings present, in extremely lifelike poses, over 1,000 species of animals. One of the most extensive pictorial sourcebooks of its kind. Captions. Index. 284pp. 9 × 12.   23766-4 Pa. $12.95

CELTIC ART: The Methods of Construction, George Bain. Simple geometric techniques for making Celtic interlacements, spirals, Kells-type initials, animals, humans, etc. Over 500 illustrations. 160pp. 9 × 12. (USO)   22923-8 Pa. $9.95

AN ATLAS OF ANATOMY FOR ARTISTS, Fritz Schider. Most thorough reference work on art anatomy in the world. Hundreds of illustrations, including selections from works by Vesalius, Leonardo, Goya, Ingres, Michelangelo, others. 593 illustrations. 192pp. 7⅛ × 10¼.   20241-0 Pa. $9.95

CELTIC HAND STROKE-BY-STROKE (Irish Half-Uncial from "The Book of Kells"): An Arthur Baker Calligraphy Manual, Arthur Baker. Complete guide to creating each letter of the alphabet in distinctive Celtic manner. Covers hand position, strokes, pens, inks, paper, more. Illustrated. 48pp. 8¼ × 11.

24336-2 Pa. $3.95

EASY ORIGAMI, John Montroll. Charming collection of 32 projects (hat, cup, pelican, piano, swan, many more) specially designed for the novice origami hobbyist. Clearly illustrated easy-to-follow instructions insure that even beginning papercrafters will achieve successful results. 48pp. 8¼ × 11.   27298-2 Pa. $2.95

THE COMPLETE BOOK OF BIRDHOUSE CONSTRUCTION FOR WOOD-WORKERS, Scott D. Campbell. Detailed instructions, illustrations, tables. Also data on bird habitat and instinct patterns. Bibliography. 3 tables. 63 illustrations in 15 figures. 48pp. 5¼ × 8½.   24407-5 Pa. $1.95

BLOOMINGDALE'S ILLUSTRATED 1886 CATALOG: Fashions, Dry Goods and Housewares, Bloomingdale Brothers. Famed merchants' extremely rare catalog depicting about 1,700 products: clothing, housewares, firearms, dry goods, jewelry, more. Invaluable for dating, identifying vintage items. Also, copyright-free graphics for artists, designers. Co-published with Henry Ford Museum & Green-field Village. 160pp. 8¼ × 11.   25780-0 Pa. $9.95

HISTORIC COSTUME IN PICTURES, Braun & Schneider. Over 1,450 costumed figures in clearly detailed engravings—from dawn of civilization to end of 19th century. Captions. Many folk costumes. 256pp. 8⅜ × 11¾.   23150-X Pa. $11.95

CATALOG OF DOVER BOOKS

STICKLEY CRAFTSMAN FURNITURE CATALOGS, Gustav Stickley and L. & J. G. Stickley. Beautiful, functional furniture in two authentic catalogs from 1910. 594 illustrations, including 277 photos, show settles, rockers, armchairs, reclining chairs, bookcases, desks, tables. 183pp. 6½ × 9¼. 23838-5 Pa. $9.95

AMERICAN LOCOMOTIVES IN HISTORIC PHOTOGRAPHS: 1858 to 1949, Ron Ziel (ed.). A rare collection of 126 meticulously detailed official photographs, called "builder portraits," of American locomotives that majestically chronicle the rise of steam locomotive power in America. Introduction. Detailed captions. xi + 129pp. 9 × 12. 27393-8 Pa. $12.95

AMERICA'S LIGHTHOUSES: An Illustrated History, Francis Ross Holland, Jr. Delightfully written, profusely illustrated fact-filled survey of over 200 American lighthouses since 1716. History, anecdotes, technological advances, more. 240pp. 8 × 10¾. 25576-X Pa. $11.95

TOWARDS A NEW ARCHITECTURE, Le Corbusier. Pioneering manifesto by founder of "International School." Technical and aesthetic theories, views of industry, economics, relation of form to function, "mass-production split" and much more. Profusely illustrated. 320pp. 6⅛ × 9¼. (USO) 25023-7 Pa. $9.95

HOW THE OTHER HALF LIVES, Jacob Riis. Famous journalistic record, exposing poverty and degradation of New York slums around 1900, by major social reformer. 100 striking and influential photographs. 233pp. 10 × 7⅞. 22012-5 Pa $10.95

FRUIT KEY AND TWIG KEY TO TREES AND SHRUBS, William M. Harlow. One of the handiest and most widely used identification aids. Fruit key covers 120 deciduous and evergreen species; twig key 160 deciduous species. Easily used. Over 300 photographs. 126pp. 5⅜ × 8½. 20511-8 Pa. $3.95

COMMON BIRD SONGS, Dr. Donald J. Borror. Songs of 60 most common U.S. birds: robins, sparrows, cardinals, bluejays, finches, more—arranged in order of increasing complexity. Up to 9 variations of songs of each species. Cassette and manual 99911-4 $8.95

ORCHIDS AS HOUSE PLANTS, Rebecca Tyson Northen. Grow cattleyas and many other kinds of orchids—in a window, in a case, or under artificial light. 63 illustrations. 148pp. 5⅜ × 8½. 23261-1 Pa. $4.95

MONSTER MAZES, Dave Phillips. Masterful mazes at four levels of difficulty. Avoid deadly perils and evil creatures to find magical treasures. Solutions for all 32 exciting illustrated puzzles. 48pp. 8¼ × 11. 26005-4 Pa. $2.95

MOZART'S DON GIOVANNI (DOVER OPERA LIBRETTO SERIES), Wolfgang Amadeus Mozart. Introduced and translated by Ellen H. Bleiler. Standard Italian libretto, with complete English translation. Convenient and thoroughly portable—an ideal companion for reading along with a recording or the performance itself. Introduction. List of characters. Plot summary. 121pp. 5¼ × 8½. 24944-1 Pa. $2.95

TECHNICAL MANUAL AND DICTIONARY OF CLASSICAL BALLET, Gail Grant. Defines, explains, comments on steps, movements, poses and concepts. 15-page pictorial section. Basic book for student, viewer. 127pp. 5⅜ × 8½. 21843-0 Pa. $4.95

BRASS INSTRUMENTS: Their History and Development, Anthony Baines. Authoritative, updated survey of the evolution of trumpets, trombones, bugles, cornets, French horns, tubas and other brass wind instruments. Over 140 illustrations and 48 music examples. Corrected and updated by author. New preface. Bibliography. 320pp. 5⅜ × 8½.   27574-4 Pa. $9.95

HOLLYWOOD GLAMOR PORTRAITS, John Kobal (ed.). 145 photos from 1926–49. Harlow, Gable, Bogart, Bacall; 94 stars in all. Full background on photographers, technical aspects. 160pp. 8⅜ × 11¼.   23352-9 Pa. $11.95

MAX AND MORITZ, Wilhelm Busch. Great humor classic in both German and English. Also 10 other works: "Cat and Mouse," "Plisch and Plumm," etc. 216pp. 5⅜ × 8½.   20181-3 Pa. $5.95

THE RAVEN AND OTHER FAVORITE POEMS, Edgar Allan Poe. Over 40 of the author's most memorable poems: "The Bells," "Ulalume," "Israfel," "To Helen," "The Conqueror Worm," "Eldorado," "Annabel Lee," many more. Alphabetic lists of titles and first lines. 64pp. 5³⁄₁₆ × 8¼.   26685-0 Pa. $1.00

SEVEN SCIENCE FICTION NOVELS, H. G. Wells. The standard collection of the great novels. Complete, unabridged. First Men in the Moon, Island of Dr. Moreau, War of the Worlds, Food of the Gods, Invisible Man, Time Machine, In the Days of the Comet. Total of 1,015pp. 5⅜ × 8½. (USO)   20264-X Clothbd. $29.95

AMULETS AND SUPERSTITIONS, E. A. Wallis Budge. Comprehensive discourse on origin, powers of amulets in many ancient cultures: Arab, Persian, Babylonian, Assyrian, Egyptian, Gnostic, Hebrew, Phoenician, Syriac, etc. Covers cross, swastika, crucifix, seals, rings, stones, etc. 584pp. 5⅜ × 8½. 23573-4 Pa. $12.95

RUSSIAN STORIES/PYCCKNE PACCKA3bl: A Dual-Language Book, edited by Gleb Struve. Twelve tales by such masters as Chekhov, Tolstoy, Dostoevsky, Pushkin, others. Excellent word-for-word English translations on facing pages, plus teaching and study aids, Russian/English vocabulary, biographical/critical introductions, more. 416pp. 5⅜ × 8½.   26244-8 Pa. $8.95

PHILADELPHIA THEN AND NOW: 60 Sites Photographed in the Past and Present, Kenneth Finkel and Susan Oyama. Rare photographs of City Hall, Logan Square, Independence Hall, Betsy Ross House, other landmarks juxtaposed with contemporary views. Captures changing face of historic city. Introduction. Captions. 128pp. 8¼ × 11.   25790-8 Pa. $9.95

AIA ARCHITECTURAL GUIDE TO NASSAU AND SUFFOLK COUNTIES, LONG ISLAND, The American Institute of Architects, Long Island Chapter, and the Society for the Preservation of Long Island Antiquities. Comprehensive, well-researched and generously illustrated volume brings to life over three centuries of Long Island's great architectural heritage. More than 240 photographs with authoritative, extensively detailed captions. 176pp. 8¼ × 11.   26946-9 Pa. $14.95

NORTH AMERICAN INDIAN LIFE: Customs and Traditions of 23 Tribes, Elsie Clews Parsons (ed.). 27 fictionalized essays by noted anthropologists examine religion, customs, government, additional facets of life among the Winnebago, Crow, Zuni, Eskimo, other tribes. 480pp. 6⅛ × 9¼.   27377-6 Pa. $10.95

FRANK LLOYD WRIGHT'S HOLLYHOCK HOUSE, Donald Hoffmann. Lavishly illustrated, carefully documented study of one of Wright's most controversial residential designs. Over 120 photographs, floor plans, elevations, etc. Detailed perceptive text by noted Wright scholar. Index. 128pp. 9¼ × 10¾.
27133-1 Pa. $11.95

THE MALE AND FEMALE FIGURE IN MOTION: 60 Classic Photographic Sequences, Eadweard Muybridge. 60 true-action photographs of men and women walking, running, climbing, bending, turning, etc., reproduced from rare 19th-century masterpiece. vi + 121pp. 9 × 12. 24745-7 Pa. $10.95

1001 QUESTIONS ANSWERED ABOUT THE SEASHORE, N. J. Berrill and Jacquelyn Berrill. Queries answered about dolphins, sea snails, sponges, starfish, fishes, shore birds, many others. Covers appearance, breeding, growth, feeding, much more. 305pp. 5¼ × 8¼. 23366-9 Pa. $7.95

GUIDE TO OWL WATCHING IN NORTH AMERICA, Donald S. Heintzelman. Superb guide offers complete data and descriptions of 19 species: barn owl, screech owl, snowy owl, many more. Expert coverage of owl-watching equipment, conservation, migrations and invasions, etc. Guide to observing sites. 84 illustrations. xiii + 193pp. 5⅜ × 8½. 27344-X Pa. $8.95

MEDICINAL AND OTHER USES OF NORTH AMERICAN PLANTS: A Historical Survey with Special Reference to the Eastern Indian Tribes, Charlotte Erichsen-Brown. Chronological historical citations document 500 years of usage of plants, trees, shrubs native to eastern Canada, northeastern U.S. Also complete identifying information. 343 illustrations. 544pp. 6½ × 9¼. 25951-X Pa. $12.95

STORYBOOK MAZES, Dave Phillips. 23 stories and mazes on two-page spreads: Wizard of Oz, Treasure Island, Robin Hood, etc. Solutions. 64pp. 8¼ × 11.
23628-5 Pa. $2.95

NEGRO FOLK MUSIC, U.S.A., Harold Courlander. Noted folklorist's scholarly yet readable analysis of rich and varied musical tradition. Includes authentic versions of over 40 folk songs. Valuable bibliography and discography. xi + 324pp. 5⅜ × 8½. 27350-4 Pa. $7.95

MOVIE-STAR PORTRAITS OF THE FORTIES, John Kobal (ed.). 163 glamor, studio photos of 106 stars of the 1940s: Rita Hayworth, Ava Gardner, Marlon Brando, Clark Gable, many more. 176pp. 8⅜ × 11¼. 23546-7 Pa. $11.95

BENCHLEY LOST AND FOUND, Robert Benchley. Finest humor from early 30s, about pet peeves, child psychologists, post office and others. Mostly unavailable elsewhere. 73 illustrations by Peter Arno and others. 183pp. 5⅜ × 8½.
22410-4 Pa. $5.95

YEKL and THE IMPORTED BRIDEGROOM AND OTHER STORIES OF YIDDISH NEW YORK, Abraham Cahan. Film Hester Street based on Yekl (1896). Novel, other stories among first about Jewish immigrants on N.Y.'s East Side. 240pp. 5⅜ × 8½. 22427-9 Pa. $6.95

SELECTED POEMS, Walt Whitman. Generous sampling from *Leaves of Grass*. Twenty-four poems include "I Hear America Singing," "Song of the Open Road," "I Sing the Body Electric," "When Lilacs Last in the Dooryard Bloom'd," "O Captain! My Captain!"—all reprinted from an authoritative edition. Lists of titles and first lines. 128pp. 5³⁄₁₆ × 8¼. 26878-0 Pa. $1.00

THE BEST TALES OF HOFFMANN, E. T. A. Hoffmann. 10 of Hoffmann's most important stories: "Nutcracker and the King of Mice," "The Golden Flowerpot," etc. 458pp. 5⅜ × 8½. 21793-0 Pa. $8.95

FROM FETISH TO GOD IN ANCIENT EGYPT, E. A. Wallis Budge. Rich detailed survey of Egyptian conception of "God" and gods, magic, cult of animals, Osiris, more. Also, superb English translations of hymns and legends. 240 illustrations. 545pp. 5⅜ × 8½. 25803-3 Pa. $11.95

FRENCH STORIES/CONTES FRANÇAIS: A Dual-Language Book, Wallace Fowlie. Ten stories by French masters, Voltaire to Camus: "Micromegas" by Voltaire; "The Atheist's Mass" by Balzac; "Minuet" by de Maupassant; "The Guest" by Camus, six more. Excellent English translations on facing pages. Also French-English vocabulary list, exercises, more. 352pp. 5⅜ × 8½. 26443-2 Pa. $8.95

CHICAGO AT THE TURN OF THE CENTURY IN PHOTOGRAPHS: 122 Historic Views from the Collections of the Chicago Historical Society, Larry A. Viskochil. Rare large-format prints offer detailed views of City Hall, State Street, the Loop, Hull House, Union Station, many other landmarks, circa 1904–1913. Introduction. Captions. Maps. 144pp. 9⅜ × 12¼. 24656-6 Pa. $12.95

OLD BROOKLYN IN EARLY PHOTOGRAPHS, 1865–1929, William Lee Younger. Luna Park, Gravesend race track, construction of Grand Army Plaza, moving of Hotel Brighton, etc. 157 previously unpublished photographs. 165pp. 8⅞ × 11¾. 23587-4 Pa. $13.95

THE MYTHS OF THE NORTH AMERICAN INDIANS, Lewis Spence. Rich anthology of the myths and legends of the Algonquins, Iroquois, Pawnees and Sioux, prefaced by an extensive historical and ethnological commentary. 36 illustrations. 480pp. 5⅜ × 8½. 25967-6 Pa. $8.95

AN ENCYCLOPEDIA OF BATTLES: Accounts of Over 1,560 Battles from 1479 B.C. to the Present, David Eggenberger. Essential details of every major battle in recorded history from the first battle of Megiddo in 1479 B.C. to Grenada in 1984. List of Battle Maps. New Appendix covering the years 1967–1984. Index. 99 illustrations. 544pp. 6½ × 9¼. 24913-1 Pa. $14.95

SAILING ALONE AROUND THE WORLD, Captain Joshua Slocum. First man to sail around the world, alone, in small boat. One of great feats of seamanship told in delightful manner. 67 illustrations. 294pp. 5⅜ × 8½. 20326-3 Pa. $5.95

ANARCHISM AND OTHER ESSAYS, Emma Goldman. Powerful, penetrating, prophetic essays on direct action, role of minorities, prison reform, puritan hypocrisy, violence, etc. 271pp. 5⅜ × 8½. 22484-8 Pa. $5.95

MYTHS OF THE HINDUS AND BUDDHISTS, Ananda K. Coomaraswamy and Sister Nivedita. Great stories of the epics; deeds of Krishna, Shiva, taken from puranas, Vedas, folk tales; etc. 32 illustrations. 400pp. 5⅜ × 8½. 21759-0 Pa. $9.95

BEYOND PSYCHOLOGY, Otto Rank. Fear of death, desire of immortality, nature of sexuality, social organization, creativity, according to Rankian system. 291pp. 5⅜ × 8½. 20485-5 Pa. $8.95

A THEOLOGICO-POLITICAL TREATISE, Benedict Spinoza. Also contains unfinished Political Treatise. Great classic on religious liberty, theory of government on common consent. R. Elwes translation. Total of 421pp. 5⅜ × 8½. 20249-6 Pa. $8.95

MY BONDAGE AND MY FREEDOM, Frederick Douglass. Born a slave, Douglass became outspoken force in antislavery movement. The best of Douglass' autobiographies. Graphic description of slave life. 464pp. 5⅜ × 8½.   22457-0 Pa. $8.95

FOLLOWING THE EQUATOR: A Journey Around the World, Mark Twain. Fascinating humorous account of 1897 voyage to Hawaii, Australia, India, New Zealand, etc. Ironic, bemused reports on peoples, customs, climate, flora and fauna, politics, much more. 197 illustrations. 720pp. 5⅜ × 8½.   26113-1 Pa. $15.95

THE PEOPLE CALLED SHAKERS, Edward D. Andrews. Definitive study of Shakers: origins, beliefs, practices, dances, social organization, furniture and crafts, etc. 33 illustrations. 351pp. 5⅜ × 8½.   21081-2 Pa. $8.95

THE MYTHS OF GREECE AND ROME, H. A. Guerber. A classic of mythology, generously illustrated, long prized for its simple, graphic, accurate retelling of the principal myths of Greece and Rome, and for its commentary on their origins and significance. With 64 illustrations by Michelangelo, Raphael, Titian, Rubens, Canova, Bernini and others. 480pp. 5⅜ × 8½.   27584-1 Pa. $9.95

PSYCHOLOGY OF MUSIC, Carl E. Seashore. Classic work discusses music as a medium from psychological viewpoint. Clear treatment of physical acoustics, auditory apparatus, sound perception, development of musical skills, nature of musical feeling, host of other topics. 88 figures. 408pp. 5⅜ × 8½.   21851-1 Pa. $9.95

THE PHILOSOPHY OF HISTORY, Georg W. Hegel. Great classic of Western thought develops concept that history is not chance but rational process, the evolution of freedom. 457pp. 5⅜ × 8½.   20112-0 Pa. $9.95

THE BOOK OF TEA, Kakuzo Okakura. Minor classic of the Orient: entertaining, charming explanation, interpretation of traditional Japanese culture in terms of tea ceremony. 94pp. 5⅜ × 8½.   20070-1 Pa. $3.95

LIFE IN ANCIENT EGYPT, Adolf Erman. Fullest, most thorough, detailed older account with much not in more recent books, domestic life, religion, magic, medicine, commerce, much more. Many illustrations reproduce tomb paintings, carvings, hieroglyphs, etc. 597pp. 5⅜ × 8½.   22632-8 Pa. $10.95

SUNDIALS, Their Theory and Construction, Albert Waugh. Far and away the best, most thorough coverage of ideas, mathematics concerned, types, construction, adjusting anywhere. Simple, nontechnical treatment allows even children to build several of these dials. Over 100 illustrations. 230pp. 5⅜ × 8½.   22947-5 Pa. $7.95

DYNAMICS OF FLUIDS IN POROUS MEDIA, Jacob Bear. For advanced students of ground water hydrology, soil mechanics and physics, drainage and irrigation engineering, and more. 335 illustrations. Exercises, with answers. 784pp. 6⅛ × 9¼.   65675-6 Pa. $19.95

SONGS OF EXPERIENCE: Facsimile Reproduction with 26 Plates in Full Color, William Blake. 26 full-color plates from a rare 1826 edition. Includes "The Tyger," "London," "Holy Thursday," and other poems. Printed text of poems. 48pp. 5¼ × 7.   24636-1 Pa. $4.95

OLD-TIME VIGNETTES IN FULL COLOR, Carol Belanger Grafton (ed.). Over 390 charming, often sentimental illustrations, selected from archives of Victorian graphics—pretty women posing, children playing, food, flowers, kittens and puppies, smiling cherubs, birds and butterflies, much more. All copyright-free. 48pp. 9¼ × 12¼.   27269-9 Pa. $5.95

PERSPECTIVE FOR ARTISTS, Rex Vicat Cole. Depth, perspective of sky and sea, shadows, much more, not usually covered. 391 diagrams, 81 reproductions of drawings and paintings. 279pp. 5⅜ × 8½. 22487-2 Pa. $6.95

DRAWING THE LIVING FIGURE, Joseph Sheppard. Innovative approach to artistic anatomy focuses on specifics of surface anatomy, rather than muscles and bones. Over 170 drawings of live models in front, back and side views, and in widely varying poses. Accompanying diagrams. 177 illustrations. Introduction. Index. 144pp. 8⅜ × 11¼. **26723-7 Pa. $8.95**

GOTHIC AND OLD ENGLISH ALPHABETS: 100 Complete Fonts, Dan X. Solo. Add power, elegance to posters, signs, other graphics with 100 stunning copyright-free alphabets: Blackstone, Dolbey, Germania, 97 more—including many lower-case, numerals, punctuation marks. 104pp. 8⅛ × 11. **24695-7 Pa. $8.95**

HOW TO DO BEADWORK, Mary White. Fundamental book on craft from simple projects to five-bead chains and woven works. 106 illustrations. 142pp. 5⅜ × 8. 20697-1 Pa. $4.95

THE BOOK OF WOOD CARVING, Charles Marshall Sayers. Finest book for beginners discusses fundamentals and offers 34 designs. "Absolutely first rate . . . well thought out and well executed."—E. J. Tangerman. 118pp. 7¾ × 10⅝. 23654-4 Pa. $5.95

ILLUSTRATED CATALOG OF CIVIL WAR MILITARY GOODS: Union Army Weapons, Insignia, Uniform Accessories, and Other Equipment, Schuyler, Hartley, and Graham. Rare, profusely illustrated 1846 catalog includes Union Army uniform and dress regulations, arms and ammunition, coats, insignia, flags, swords, rifles, etc. 226 illustrations. 160pp. 9 × 12. 24939-5 Pa. $10.95

WOMEN'S FASHIONS OF THE EARLY 1900s: An Unabridged Republication of "New York Fashions, 1909," National Cloak & Suit Co. Rare catalog of mail-order fashions documents women's and children's clothing styles shortly after the turn of the century. Captions offer full descriptions, prices. Invaluable resource for fashion, costume historians. Approximately 725 illustrations. 128pp. 8⅜ × 11¼. **27276-1 Pa. $11.95**

THE 1912 AND 1915 GUSTAV STICKLEY FURNITURE CATALOGS, Gustav Stickley. With over 200 detailed illustrations and descriptions, these two catalogs are essential reading and reference materials and identification guides for Stickley furniture. Captions cite materials, dimensions and prices. 112pp. 6½ × 9¼. 26676-1 Pa. $9.95

EARLY AMERICAN LOCOMOTIVES, John H. White, Jr. Finest locomotive engravings from early 19th century: historical (1804–74), main-line (after 1870), special, foreign, etc. 147 plates. 142pp. 11⅜ × 8¼. **22772-3 Pa. $10.95**

THE TALL SHIPS OF TODAY IN PHOTOGRAPHS, Frank O. Braynard. Lavishly illustrated tribute to nearly 100 majestic contemporary sailing vessels: Amerigo Vespucci, Clearwater, Constitution, Eagle, Mayflower, Sea Cloud, Victory, many more. Authoritative captions provide statistics, background on each ship. 190 black-and-white photographs and illustrations. Introduction. 128pp. 8⅞ × 11¾. **27163-3 Pa. $13.95**

EARLY NINETEENTH-CENTURY CRAFTS AND TRADES, Peter Stockham (ed.). Extremely rare 1807 volume describes to youngsters the crafts and trades of the day: brickmaker, weaver, dressmaker, bookbinder, ropemaker, saddler, many more. Quaint prose, charming illustrations for each craft. 20 black-and-white line illustrations. 192pp. 4⅜ × 6. 27293-1 Pa. $4.95

VICTORIAN FASHIONS AND COSTUMES FROM HARPER'S BAZAR, 1867–1898, Stella Blum (ed.). Day costumes, evening wear, sports clothes, shoes, hats, other accessories in over 1,000 detailed engravings. 320pp. 9⅜ × 12¼. 22990-4 Pa. $13.95

GUSTAV STICKLEY, THE CRAFTSMAN, Mary Ann Smith. Superb study surveys broad scope of Stickley's achievement, especially in architecture. Design philosophy, rise and fall of the Craftsman empire, descriptions and floor plans for many Craftsman houses, more. 86 black-and-white halftones. 31 line illustrations. Introduction. 208pp. 6½ × 9¼. 27210-9 Pa. $9.95

THE LONG ISLAND RAIL ROAD IN EARLY PHOTOGRAPHS, Ron Ziel. Over 220 rare photos, informative text document origin (1844) and development of rail service on Long Island. Vintage views of early trains, locomotives, stations, passengers, crews, much more. Captions. 8⅞ × 11¾. 26301-0 Pa. $13.95

THE BOOK OF OLD SHIPS: From Egyptian Galleys to Clipper Ships, Henry B. Culver. Superb, authoritative history of sailing vessels, with 80 magnificent line illustrations. Galley, bark, caravel, longship, whaler, many more. Detailed, informative text on each vessel by noted naval historian. Introduction. 256pp. 5⅜ × 8½. 27332-6 Pa. $6.95

TEN BOOKS ON ARCHITECTURE, Vitruvius. The most important book ever written on architecture. Early Roman aesthetics, technology, classical orders, site selection, all other aspects. Morgan translation. 331pp. 5⅜ × 8½. 20645-9 Pa. $8.95

THE HUMAN FIGURE IN MOTION, Eadweard Muybridge. More than 4,500 stopped-action photos, in action series, showing undraped men, women, children jumping, lying down, throwing, sitting, wrestling, carrying, etc. 390pp. 7⅞ × 10⅝. 20204-6 Clothbd. $24.95

TREES OF THE EASTERN AND CENTRAL UNITED STATES AND CANADA, William M. Harlow. Best one-volume guide to 140 trees. Full descriptions, woodlore, range, etc. Over 600 illustrations. Handy size. 288pp. 4½ × 6⅜. 20395-6 Pa. $5.95

SONGS OF WESTERN BIRDS, Dr. Donald J. Borror. Complete song and call repertoire of 60 western species, including flycatchers, juncoes, cactus wrens, many more—includes fully illustrated booklet. Cassette and manual 99913-0 $8.95

GROWING AND USING HERBS AND SPICES, Milo Miloradovich. Versatile handbook provides all the information needed for cultivation and use of all the herbs and spices available in North America. 4 illustrations. Index. Glossary. 236pp. 5⅜ × 8½. 25058-X Pa. $6.95

BIG BOOK OF MAZES AND LABYRINTHS, Walter Shepherd. 50 mazes and labyrinths in all—classical, solid, ripple, and more—in one great volume. Perfect inexpensive puzzler for clever youngsters. Full solutions. 112pp. 8⅛ × 11. 22951-3 Pa. $4.95

PIANO TUNING, J. Cree Fischer. Clearest, best book for beginner, amateur. Simple repairs, raising dropped notes, tuning by easy method of flattened fifths. No previous skills needed. 4 illustrations. 201pp. 5⅜ × 8½. 23267-0 Pa. $5.95

A SOURCE BOOK IN THEATRICAL HISTORY, A. M. Nagler. Contemporary observers on acting, directing, make-up, costuming, stage props, machinery, scene design, from Ancient Greece to Chekhov. 611pp. 5⅜ × 8½. 20515-0 Pa. $11.95

THE COMPLETE NONSENSE OF EDWARD LEAR, Edward Lear. All nonsense limericks, zany alphabets, Owl and Pussycat, songs, nonsense botany, etc., illustrated by Lear. Total of 320pp. 5⅜ × 8½. (USO) 20167-8 Pa. $6.95

VICTORIAN PARLOUR POETRY: An Annotated Anthology, Michael R. Turner. 117 gems by Longfellow, Tennyson, Browning, many lesser-known poets. "The Village Blacksmith," "Curfew Must Not Ring Tonight," "Only a Baby Small," dozens more, often difficult to find elsewhere. Index of poets, titles, first lines. xxiii + 325pp. 5⅜ × 8¼. 27044-0 Pa. $8.95

DUBLINERS, James Joyce. Fifteen stories offer vivid, tightly focused observations of the lives of Dublin's poorer classes. At least one, "The Dead," is considered a masterpiece. Reprinted complete and unabridged from standard edition. 160pp. 5³⁄₁₆ × 8¼. 26870-5 Pa. $1.00

THE HAUNTED MONASTERY and THE CHINESE MAZE MURDERS, Robert van Gulik. Two full novels by van Gulik, set in 7th-century China, continue adventures of Judge Dee and his companions. An evil Taoist monastery, seemingly supernatural events; overgrown topiary maze hides strange crimes. 27 illustrations. 328pp. 5⅜ × 8½. 23502-5 Pa. $7.95

THE BOOK OF THE SACRED MAGIC OF ABRAMELIN THE MAGE, translated by S. MacGregor Mathers. Medieval manuscript of ceremonial magic. Basic document in Aleister Crowley, Golden Dawn groups. 268pp. 5⅜ × 8½. 23211-5 Pa. $8.95

NEW RUSSIAN-ENGLISH AND ENGLISH-RUSSIAN DICTIONARY, M. A. O'Brien. This is a remarkably handy Russian dictionary, containing a surprising amount of information, including over 70,000 entries. 366pp. 4½ × 6⅛. 20208-9 Pa. $9.95

HISTORIC HOMES OF THE AMERICAN PRESIDENTS, Second, Revised Edition, Irvin Haas. A traveler's guide to American Presidential homes, most open to the public, depicting and describing homes occupied by every American President from George Washington to George Bush. With visiting hours, admission charges, travel routes. 175 photographs. Index. 160pp. 8¼ × 11. 26751-2 Pa. $10.95

NEW YORK IN THE FORTIES, Andreas Feininger. 162 brilliant photographs by the well-known photographer, formerly with *Life* magazine. Commuters, shoppers, Times Square at night, much else from city at its peak. Captions by John von Hartz. 181pp. 9¼ × 10¾. 23585-8 Pa. $12.95

INDIAN SIGN LANGUAGE, William Tomkins. Over 525 signs developed by Sioux and other tribes. Written instructions and diagrams. Also 290 pictographs. 111pp. 6⅛ × 9¼. 22029-X Pa. $3.50

ANATOMY: A Complete Guide for Artists, Joseph Sheppard. A master of figure drawing shows artists how to render human anatomy convincingly. Over 460 illustrations. 224pp. 8⅜ × 11¼. 27279-6 Pa. $10.95

MEDIEVAL CALLIGRAPHY: Its History and Technique, Marc Drogin. Spirited history, comprehensive instruction manual covers 13 styles (ca. 4th century thru 15th). Excellent photographs; directions for duplicating medieval techniques with modern tools. 224pp. 8⅜ × 11¼. 26142-5 Pa. $11.95

DRIED FLOWERS: How to Prepare Them, Sarah Whitlock and Martha Rankin. Complete instructions on how to use silica gel, meal and borax, perlite aggregate, sand and borax, glycerine and water to create attractive permanent flower arrangements. 12 illustrations. 32pp. 5⅜ × 8½. 21802-3 Pa. $1.00

EASY-TO-MAKE BIRD FEEDERS FOR WOODWORKERS, Scott D. Campbell. Detailed, simple-to-use guide for designing, constructing, caring for and using feeders. Text, illustrations for 12 classic and contemporary designs. 96pp. 5⅜ × 8½. 25847-5 Pa. $2.95

OLD-TIME CRAFTS AND TRADES, Peter Stockham. An 1807 book created to teach children about crafts and trades open to them as future careers. It describes in detailed, nontechnical terms 24 different occupations, among them coachmaker, gardener, hairdresser, lacemaker, shoemaker, wheelwright, copper-plate printer, milliner, trunkmaker, merchant and brewer. Finely detailed engravings illustrate each occupation. 192pp. 4⅝ × 6. 27398-9 Pa. $4.95

THE HISTORY OF UNDERCLOTHES, C. Willett Cunnington and Phyllis Cunnington. Fascinating, well-documented survey covering six centuries of English undergarments, enhanced with over 100 illustrations: 12th-century laced-up bodice, footed long drawers (1795), 19th-century bustles, 19th-century corsets for men, Victorian "bust improvers," much more. 272pp. 5⅜ × 8¼. 27124-2 Pa. $9.95

ARTS AND CRAFTS FURNITURE: The Complete Brooks Catalog of 1912, Brooks Manufacturing Co. Photos and detailed descriptions of more than 150 now very collectible furniture designs from the Arts and Crafts movement depict davenports, settees, buffets, desks, tables, chairs, bedsteads, dressers and more, all built of solid, quarter-sawed oak. Invaluable for students and enthusiasts of antiques, Americana and the decorative arts. 80pp. 6½ × 9¼. 27471-3 Pa. $7.95

HOW WE INVENTED THE AIRPLANE: An Illustrated History, Orville Wright. Fascinating firsthand account covers early experiments, construction of planes and motors, first flights, much more. Introduction and commentary by Fred C. Kelly. 76 photographs. 96pp. 8¼ × 11. 25662-6 Pa. $8.95

THE ARTS OF THE SAILOR: Knotting, Splicing and Ropework, Hervey Garrett Smith. Indispensable shipboard reference covers tools, basic knots and useful hitches; handsewing and canvas work, more. Over 100 illustrations. Delightful reading for sea lovers. 256pp. 5⅜ × 8½. 26440-8 Pa. $7.95

FRANK LLOYD WRIGHT'S FALLINGWATER: The House and Its History, Second, Revised Edition, Donald Hoffmann. A total revision—both in text and illustrations—of the standard document on Fallingwater, the boldest, most personal architectural statement of Wright's mature years, updated with valuable new material from the recently opened Frank Lloyd Wright Archives. "Fascinating"—*The New York Times*. 116 illustrations. 128pp. 9¼ × 10¾. 27430-6 Pa. $10.95

CATALOG OF DOVER BOOKS

PHOTOGRAPHIC SKETCHBOOK OF THE CIVIL WAR, Alexander Gardner. 100 photos taken on field during the Civil War. Famous shots of Manassas, Harper's Ferry, Lincoln, Richmond, slave pens, etc. 244pp. 10⅝ × 8¼.
22731-6 Pa. $9.95

FIVE ACRES AND INDEPENDENCE, Maurice G. Kains. Great back-to-the-land classic explains basics of self-sufficient farming. The one book to get. 95 illustrations. 397pp. 5⅜ × 8½.
20974-1 Pa. $7.95

SONGS OF EASTERN BIRDS, Dr. Donald J. Borror. Songs and calls of 60 species most common to eastern U.S.: warblers, woodpeckers, flycatchers, thrushes, larks, many more in high-quality recording.
Cassette and manual 99912-2 $8.95

A MODERN HERBAL, Margaret Grieve. Much the fullest, most exact, most useful compilation of herbal material. Gigantic alphabetical encyclopedia, from aconite to zedoary, gives botanical information, medical properties, folklore, economic uses, much else. Indispensable to serious reader. 161 illustrations. 888pp. 6½ × 9¼.
2-vol. set. (USO)
Vol. I: 22798-7 Pa. $9.95
Vol. II: 22799-5 Pa. $9.95

HIDDEN TREASURE MAZE BOOK, Dave Phillips. Solve 34 challenging mazes accompanied by heroic tales of adventure. Evil dragons, people-eating plants, bloodthirsty giants, many more dangerous adversaries lurk at every twist and turn. 34 mazes, stories, solutions. 48pp. 8¼ × 11.
24566-7 Pa. $2.95

LETTERS OF W. A. MOZART, Wolfgang A. Mozart. Remarkable letters show bawdy wit, humor, imagination, musical insights, contemporary musical world; includes some letters from Leopold Mozart. 276pp. 5⅜ × 8½.
22859-2 Pa. $7.95

BASIC PRINCIPLES OF CLASSICAL BALLET, Agrippina Vaganova. Great Russian theoretician, teacher explains methods for teaching classical ballet. 118 illustrations. 175pp. 5⅜ × 8½.
22036-2 Pa. $4.95

THE JUMPING FROG, Mark Twain. Revenge edition. The original story of The Celebrated Jumping Frog of Calaveras County, a hapless French translation, and Twain's hilarious "retranslation" from the French. 12 illustrations. 66pp. 5⅜ × 8½.
22686-7 Pa. $3.95

BEST REMEMBERED POEMS, Martin Gardner (ed.). The 126 poems in this superb collection of 19th- and 20th-century British and American verse range from Shelley's "To a Skylark" to the impassioned "Renascence" of Edna St. Vincent Millay and to Edward Lear's whimsical "The Owl and the Pussycat." 224pp. 5⅜ × 8½.
27165-X Pa. $4.95

COMPLETE SONNETS, William Shakespeare. Over 150 exquisite poems deal with love, friendship, the tyranny of time, beauty's evanescence, death and other themes in language of remarkable power, precision and beauty. Glossary of archaic terms. 80pp. 5³⁄₁₆ × 8¼.
26686-9 Pa. $1.00

BODIES IN A BOOKSHOP, R. T. Campbell. Challenging mystery of blackmail and murder with ingenious plot and superbly drawn characters. In the best tradition of British suspense fiction. 192pp. 5⅜ × 8½.
24720-1 Pa. $5.95

THE WIT AND HUMOR OF OSCAR WILDE, Alvin Redman (ed.). More than 1,000 ripostes, paradoxes, wisecracks: Work is the curse of the drinking classes; I can resist everything except temptation; etc. 258pp. 5⅜ × 8½. 20602-5 Pa. $5.95

SHAKESPEARE LEXICON AND QUOTATION DICTIONARY, Alexander Schmidt. Full definitions, locations, shades of meaning in every word in plays and poems. More than 50,000 exact quotations. 1,485pp. 6½ × 9¼. 2-vol. set.
Vol. I: 22726-X Pa. $16.95
Vol. 2: 22727-8 Pa. $15.95

SELECTED POEMS, Emily Dickinson. Over 100 best-known, best-loved poems by one of America's foremost poets, reprinted from authoritative early editions. No comparable edition at this price. Index of first lines. 64pp. 5³⁄₁₆ × 8¼.
26466-1 Pa. $1.00

CELEBRATED CASES OF JUDGE DEE (DEE GOONG AN), translated by Robert van Gulik. Authentic 18th-century Chinese detective novel; Dee and associates solve three interlocked cases. Led to van Gulik's own stories with same characters. Extensive introduction. 9 illustrations. 237pp. 5⅜ × 8½.
23337-5 Pa. $6.95

THE MALLEUS MALEFICARUM OF KRAMER AND SPRENGER, translated by Montague Summers. Full text of most important witchhunter's "bible," used by both Catholics and Protestants. 278pp. 6⅝ × 10. 22802-9 Pa. $11.95

SPANISH STORIES/CUENTOS ESPAÑOLES: A Dual-Language Book, Angel Flores (ed.). Unique format offers 13 great stories in Spanish by Cervantes, Borges, others. Faithful English translations on facing pages. 352pp. 5⅜ × 8½.
25399-6 Pa. $8.95

THE CHICAGO WORLD'S FAIR OF 1893: A Photographic Record, Stanley Appelbaum (ed.). 128 rare photos show 200 buildings, Beaux-Arts architecture, Midway, original Ferris Wheel, Edison's kinetoscope, more. Architectural emphasis; full text. 116pp. 8¼ × 11. 23990-X Pa. $9.95

OLD QUEENS, N.Y., IN EARLY PHOTOGRAPHS, Vincent F. Seyfried and William Asadorian. Over 160 rare photographs of Maspeth, Jamaica, Jackson Heights, and other areas. Vintage views of DeWitt Clinton mansion, 1939 World's Fair and more. Captions. 192pp. 8⅞ × 11. 26358-4 Pa. $12.95

CAPTURED BY THE INDIANS: 15 Firsthand Accounts, 1750–1870, Frederick Drimmer. Astounding true historical accounts of grisly torture, bloody conflicts, relentless pursuits, miraculous escapes and more, by people who lived to tell the tale. 384pp. 5⅜ × 8½. 24901-8 Pa. $8.95

THE WORLD'S GREAT SPEECHES, Lewis Copeland and Lawrence W. Lamm (eds.). Vast collection of 278 speeches of Greeks to 1970. Powerful and effective models; unique look at history. 842pp. 5⅜ × 8½. 20468-5 Pa. $14.95

THE BOOK OF THE SWORD, Sir Richard F. Burton. Great Victorian scholar/adventurer's eloquent, erudite history of the "queen of weapons"—from prehistory to early Roman Empire. Evolution and development of early swords, variations (sabre, broadsword, cutlass, scimitar, etc.), much more. 336pp. 6⅛ × 9¼. 25434-8 Pa. $8.95

CATALOG OF DOVER BOOKS

AUTOBIOGRAPHY: The Story of My Experiments with Truth, Mohandas K. Gandhi. Boyhood, legal studies, purification, the growth of the Satyagraha (nonviolent protest) movement. Critical, inspiring work of the man responsible for the freedom of India. 480pp. 5⅜ × 8½. (USO) 24593-4 Pa. $8.95

CELTIC MYTHS AND LEGENDS, T. W. Rolleston. Masterful retelling of Irish and Welsh stories and tales. Cuchulain, King Arthur, Deirdre, the Grail, many more. First paperback edition. 58 full-page illustrations. 512pp. 5⅜ × 8½.
26507-2 Pa. $9.95

THE PRINCIPLES OF PSYCHOLOGY, William James. Famous long course complete, unabridged. Stream of thought, time perception, memory, experimental methods; great work decades ahead of its time. 94 figures. 1,391pp. 5⅜ × 8½. 2-vol. set.
Vol. I: 20381-6 Pa. $12.95
Vol. II: 20382-4 Pa. $12.95

THE WORLD AS WILL AND REPRESENTATION, Arthur Schopenhauer. Definitive English translation of Schopenhauer's life work, correcting more than 1,000 errors, omissions in earlier translations. Translated by E. F. J. Payne. Total of 1,269pp. 5⅜ × 8½. 2-vol. set.
Vol. 1: 21761-2 Pa. $11.95
Vol. 2: 21762-0 Pa. $11.95

MAGIC AND MYSTERY IN TIBET, Madame Alexandra David-Neel. Experiences among lamas, magicians, sages, sorcerers, Bonpa wizards. A true psychic discovery. 32 illustrations. 321pp. 5⅜ × 8½. (USO) 22682-4 Pa. $8.95

THE EGYPTIAN BOOK OF THE DEAD, E. A. Wallis Budge. Complete reproduction of Ani's papyrus, finest ever found. Full hieroglyphic text, interlinear transliteration, word-for-word translation, smooth translation. 533pp. 6½ × 9¼.
21866-X Pa. $9.95

MATHEMATICS FOR THE NONMATHEMATICIAN, Morris Kline. Detailed, college-level treatment of mathematics in cultural and historical context, with numerous exercises. Recommended Reading Lists. Tables. Numerous figures. 641pp. 5⅜ × 8½. 24823-2 Pa. $11.95

THEORY OF WING SECTIONS: Including a Summary of Airfoil Data, Ira H. Abbott and A. E. von Doenhoff. Concise compilation of subsonic aerodynamic characteristics of NACA wing sections, plus description of theory. 350pp. of tables. 693pp. 5⅜ × 8½. 60586-8 Pa. $14.95

THE RIME OF THE ANCIENT MARINER, Gustave Doré, S. T. Coleridge. Doré's finest work; 34 plates capture moods, subtleties of poem. Flawless full-size reproductions printed on facing pages with authoritative text of poem. "Beautiful. Simply beautiful."—*Publisher's Weekly.* 77pp. 9¼ × 12. 22305-1 Pa. $6.95

NORTH AMERICAN INDIAN DESIGNS FOR ARTISTS AND CRAFTS-PEOPLE, Eva Wilson. Over 360 authentic copyright-free designs adapted from Navajo blankets, Hopi pottery, Sioux buffalo hides, more. Geometrics, symbolic figures, plant and animal motifs, etc. 128pp. 8⅜ × 11. (EUK) 25341-4 Pa. $7.95

SCULPTURE: Principles and Practice, Louis Slobodkin. Step-by-step approach to clay, plaster, metals, stone; classical and modern. 253 drawings, photos. 255pp. 8⅛ × 11. 22960-2 Pa. $10.95

CATALOG OF DOVER BOOKS

THE INFLUENCE OF SEA POWER UPON HISTORY, 1660–1783, A. T. Mahan. Influential classic of naval history and tactics still used as text in war colleges. First paperback edition. 4 maps. 24 battle plans. 640pp. 5⅜ × 8½.
25509-3 Pa. $12.95

THE STORY OF THE TITANIC AS TOLD BY ITS SURVIVORS, Jack Winocour (ed.). What it was really like. Panic, despair, shocking inefficiency, and a little heroism. More thrilling than any fictional account. 26 illustrations. 320pp. 5⅜ × 8½.
20610-6 Pa. $8.95

FAIRY AND FOLK TALES OF THE IRISH PEASANTRY, William Butler Yeats (ed.). Treasury of 64 tales from the twilight world of Celtic myth and legend: "The Soul Cages," "The Kildare Pooka," "King O'Toole and his Goose," many more. Introduction and Notes by W. B. Yeats. 352pp. 5⅜ × 8½. 26941-8 Pa. $8.95

BUDDHIST MAHAYANA TEXTS, E. B. Cowell and Others (eds.). Superb, accurate translations of basic documents in Mahayana Buddhism, highly important in history of religions. The Buddha-karita of Asvaghosha, Larger Sukhavativyuha, more. 448pp. 5⅜ × 8½. 25552-2 Pa. $9.95

ONE TWO THREE . . . INFINITY: Facts and Speculations of Science, George Gamow. Great physicist's fascinating, readable overview of contemporary science: number theory, relativity, fourth dimension, entropy, genes, atomic structure, much more. 128 illustrations. Index. 352pp. 5⅜ × 8½. 25664-2 Pa. $8.95

ENGINEERING IN HISTORY, Richard Shelton Kirby, et al. Broad, nontechnical survey of history's major technological advances: birth of Greek science, industrial revolution, electricity and applied science, 20th-century automation, much more. 181 illustrations. ". . . excellent . . ."—Isis. Bibliography. vii + 530pp. 5⅜ × 8¼.
26412-2 Pa. $14.95

Prices subject to change without notice.

Available at your book dealer or write for free catalog to Dept. GI, Dover Publications, Inc., 31 East 2nd St., Mineola, N.Y. 11501. Dover publishes more than 500 books each year on science, elementary and advanced mathematics, biology, music, art, literary history, social sciences and other areas.